West Port Murders: The Story of Burke and Hare

ISBN:

ISBN-13:

CONTENTS

About The Author

L.A Mackay is a historian and author of several acclaimed books over the past decade. L.A Mackay has explored and investigated many unique topics, locales and people to fully understand and reveal the hidden secrets of them.

L.A Mackay has presented at conferences providing insight from her books and research across the country.

L.A Mackay

INTRODUCTION

I began my journey into Burke and Hare after I had moved to Scotland in 2017. I knew of the story of Burke and Hare from my visit to Edinburgh in the past, but I was desperate to know more.

In the beginning, I was not intending to write a book on their lives, I guess I was just curious and wanted to know more about them. In 2018, during a trip to the city, I decided to find a few locations, to see how they had changed over the years and if there were any signs that Burke and Hare had existed.

Through painstaking research, I will look at thousands of documents, books, old maps and much more to see what I can find out about these men. Were there other people involved in the crimes and did the right man lose his life?

Below is a small list of my research we will be looking at:

Books:

- The Trial of Wm. Burke & Helen M'Dougal – J Pratt (1829)
- West Port Murders – Thomas Ireland (1829)
- Observations on the phrenological development of Burke, Hare, and other atrocious murderers – Thomas Stone (1829)
- Old and New Edinburgh - James Grant (1880)
- The History of Burke & Hare – George Mac Gregor (1884)
- Burke & Hare – William Roughead (1921)
- Burke & Hare – Owen Dudley Edwards (1980)
- Scottish Murders – Lisa Wallis & Derek Wright (2012)
- Scottish Murderers – Judy Hamilton (2013)
- Burke & Hare - The Stentmaisters (2014)
- Bloody Scotland: Crime in 19th Century Scotland – Malcolm Archibald (2014)
- Hare: A Novel – Peter Ranscombe (2015)
- Burke Now and Then – Janet Philp (2016)

Maps:

- Map of Edinburghshire III.7 (Edinburgh) (1908)
- Map of Edinburgh - Sheet 38 (1851)
- Map of Edinburghshire III.8 (Edinburgh) (1896)
- Reduced plan of the proposed Edinburgh & Glasgow Union Canal from lock no. 10 on the Forth & Clyde Canal - Hugh Baird (1815)
- Plan showing the Forth & Clyde, Monkland, & Union Canals with the various railways - Maclure, Hugh Hough and Macdonald (1846)
- The East Central Lowlands (Stirling, Falkirk & Kilsyth) – Timothy Point (1583-96)
- Map of Edinburgh- Sheet 35 (1852)
- Google map (2020)

Reports:

- Broadside - A broadside is a large sheet of paper printed on one side only, which was usually sold for a penny. The document was made to look like a poster or advertisement. These were used to announce events, proclamations, commentary in the form of ballads, or simply advertisements.
- Newspaper Articles – Just like today, any popular story is in the newspaper for everyone to read. Some of these articles make the front page, while some are just a little section.
- Dictionary of National Biography, Volumes 1-22 – A reference book which was published from 1885
- Reports of Proceedings in the High Court of Justiciary: From 1826 to 1829 – David Syme (1829)

Documentation:

- United States Federal Censuses/ California, U.S., County Birth, Marriage, and Death Records, 1849-1980
- Australia, Births and Baptisms, 1792-1981/New South Wales, Australia, Assisted Immigrant Passenger Lists, 1828-1896
- U.S., City Directories, 1822-1995/Find a Grave Index, 1600s-Current/Newspapers.com Obituary Index, 1800s-current/Army, Register of Enlistments, 1798-1914
- UK and Ireland, Find a Grave Index, 1300s-Current
- Scotland, Select Marriages, 1561-1910/ Scotland, Select Births and Baptisms, 1564-1950
- St Cuthbert's Old Parish Marriage Register/ St Cuthbert's Old Parish Death Register
- Canongate Old Parish Marriage Register
- Ireland, Catholic Parish Registers, 1655-1915/Ireland, Civil Registration Deaths Index, 1864-1958

From the early 1300s to 1922, most of the Irish documents were destroyed in a fire. This left my research with big gaps and was the reason why I had to look elsewhere for some answers.

Most people know of the story of Edinburgh's 'grave robbers' Burke and Hare. Two Irish men, who came over to Scotland to make some money by grave-digging and selling corpses to the local teaching Doctors. But how much of this story is true?

This book will also look into what happened after these events, to the people and the change in the law. Did this change stop these crimes from happening?

EDINBURGH

Edinburgh – *"The capital of Scotland and seat of the Scottish Parliament (from 1999), in City of Edinburgh council area on the south side of the Firth of Forth: became the capital in the 15th century; castle; three universities (including University of Edinburgh, 1583)"*.

Collinsdictionary.com

The city of Edinburgh that we see today is divided up to into two sections, the old town and the new town. The old town of Edinburgh was constructed on a volcanic plug, in medieval times under the reign of King Malcolm III, King of Scotland. During his reign, he built Edinburgh Castle. Within the walls of a castle, he built a Chapel for his wife Margaret to worship in. This chapel is the oldest building in the city and can be still seen when looking around the Castle.

What is a Volcanic Plug? *"A volcanic plug or volcanic neck is a geographical formation that occurs when lava cools inside a vent of an active volcano, and the connecting deposit is eroded away. During formation of a plug, an explosive eruption can take place if rising impulsive-charged magma is trapped beneath a plug. A distinctive landform is formed if a plug is conserved because the erosion-resistant plug remains after the adjoining rock has eroded"*.

worldatlas.com

King David I, the son of King Malcolm III and Margaret decided to build Holyrood Abbey in 1128, when he began his role of King of Scotland. This was four years into his leadership as King. Holyrood Abbey is one of the oldest buildings in Edinburgh and is now a ruin. It is positioned one mile to the east of Edinburgh Castle, down the street what is now named the 'Royal Mile', which is Castle Hill, High Street and Canongate combined. In-between the castle and abbey were three mixed classes of houses, shops and public houses.

As you walk down or up the Royal Mile, you can see 81 'Closes' on either side. These closes were narrow alleyways that usually led downwards with high walls as protection for the city. Down these closes would be more housing, shops and sometimes would connect to much larger streets. The name of the closes came from people who occupied one of the buildings or a name of a trade for example Bakehouse Close, which is located at the South side of Canongate or Brodie's Close, which was named after the family home of Deacon Brodie, who was a local cabinet maker in Edinburgh.

Around this era, the Scots were constantly attacked by the English, who wanted to take over the country for themselves. The English set their sights on Edinburgh and would send their army up to Scotland to try and seize their property. This worried the people of Edinburgh, who did not want to live outside the city walls. This meant that the city became overcrowded. Quite quickly there was no more room to build houses and their only way of building more houses is on top of the buildings that already exist. These buildings are now known as the first skyscrapers, which were up to fourteen floors high.

Overcrowding was an issue due to the many infections and illnesses that we being transmitted from one person to another. In 1645, Edinburgh suffered through The Great Plague of Edinburgh, where approximately half of the city's population died. The Plague was started by fleas on rats, which were taken throughout Europe. Anyone who was bit by the insect contracted the disease and then that person was able to transmit the infection person to person until much of the population was ill.

Gravediggers found the task of burying the dead tricky, as there were too many of them. As one of the last resorts, pits were dug up where a handful of bodies were buried together at the same time. These were later known as Plague Pits. Of course, other diseases were around at this time, but it was the Plague that shut down the fully housed street, which was then built on top. One of these streets is Mary's King Close, which is now a tourist attraction, on the Royal Mile.

By the 18th century, the higher-class locals had had enough of living in the old town. It was crowded, smelly and very unhygienic. The higher society decided that they did not want to live near the lower classes and decided to move further away. This is when the New Town of Edinburgh began to form. By now King George III was in power and had to agree to any plans, that changed the city. These new plans were designed by a young man named James Craig. Craig wanted the main street of the New Town to be named St Giles, after the old church and the patron saint of Lepers, however, the King wanted the street to be named Princes Street, after his son and it has been named that ever since.

Princes Street is now the main shopping location in Edinburgh, with addition to this, hotels were built to accommodate the tourists and out of town workers. Soon a financial sector was built in the West End and a large railway station and Gallery.

To let you know how the population has increased in Edinburgh, the earliest documentation I could find was in 1755, when Edinburgh and the surrounding area of Leith housed 57,000 people. During the era that this book is written about (in the 1800s), the population had increased to 160,000 people. That is over double in approximately 75 years. Last year in 2020, the population was 537,000 in Edinburgh alone.

In the 19th Century

At the beginning of the 19th century, the United Kingdom had now combined and was ruled by one King, a man named George III. King George was based in London, England and reigned the countries from the 25th of October 1760, until his death on the 29th of January 1820.

Overcrowding was still a big issue in the Old Town during the 1800s and the area was not hygienic. Local people would empty their chamber pots into the busy roads and animals would also relieve themselves in the local area too. As you can imagine it looked and smelt awful.

The towns poorest people moved into the south vaults, which were originally designed to store stock from the local shops, but this was stopped due to the dampness and water which seeped through the walls. The vaults were eventually abandoned and the homeless and poor moved into the chambers, sleeping possibly up to thirty people in one room.

Edinburgh began to see an influx of immigration especially from Ireland, where people travelled into the city and surrounding areas, looking for jobs. If a job was available most labourers work did not pay the sufficient funds to enable people to live. This gave several people ideas to think of how they could earn more money.

After the death of King George III, his son George IV, took over the responsibility of running the United Kingdom. Four years into his reign, a fire broke out on the High Street, in the Old Town of Edinburgh. This later became known as 'The Great Fire of Edinburgh'. The fire occurred between the 15th and 17th of November 1824 and started at a seven-Storey building with a printing shop on the ground floor. The roads and closes were so narrow that the fire easily spread from one building to another. As the locals and the newly developed first fire brigade got to work and attempted to distinguish the flames, it seems that they did a good job and by the middle of the next day (16th), the fire was out.

Unfortunately, that was not the end of the tale, as it seems that the embers of the fire had been blown to the Tron Kirk and that quickly began to blaze. This lead the roof which was made of out lead to melt into the street. With that fire now under control, a third fire began to alight, this time at an eleven-Storey building in what we know now as Parliament Square. At the time of the event, the fire took place at the corner of High Street and Parliament Close. Parts of the burnt down centre were redeveloped after the fire.

By the next morning, all three of the fires were out and no more major fires had appeared, this was helped by the autumn rain that towered over the city. However, the damage to the city left up to 500 families homeless, destroying approximately 400 resident's homes was lost this included;

- On High Street, four six-storey tenements were fully lost plus upper storeys of buildings closer to the Tron Kirk were also damaged.
- On Conn's Close, two accident timber-framed tenements were destroyed completely.
- On the Old Assembly Close, four seven-storey tenements were destroyed beyond repair, as well as the Assembly Hall.
- Borthwick's Close lost six tenements.
- On the Old Fishmarket Close, four of the six-storey tenements were lost, as well as Neill & Co printworks.
- On Parliament Close, four double tenements of between seven and eleven storeys high were destroyed, including the birthplace of James Boswell.
- The office that belonged to the Edinburgh Courant newspaper was destroyed.
- A shop in Parliament Close, which was run by John Kay was destroyed.
- The Old Assembly Hall was destroyed.
- Several other printworks and offices were destroyed.

In all thirteen people lost their lives in the Great Fire of Edinburgh, including two newly recruited firemen, who had helped to put the flames out.

It took the city up to a decade to rebuild what they had lost in the fire. This included re-evaluating the high street and surrounding streets, making the buildings much shorter than what they had been and being built further apart. Many Scots saw this fire as a blessing in disguise, as more guidelines for the building were now set in place.

Anatomist

Anatomist - *"an expert in anatomy, which is the study of the structure of the body and its parts"*
Dictionary.cambridge.org

In the 19th century, Anatomists began to increase in numbers. Medical science was in its infancy and it was important to the Doctor to know how the body works and to find the cause of death.

The local Anatomists taught about their findings and would hold demonstrations, where people could pay to go along and watch them at work, which usually involves them in dissecting a body. Unfortunately, the Doctors were only permitted to use bodies that came from an executed person and could only have six a year. This left a huge hole in the market and for an Anatomist to be able to get further ahead than their competition, they needed more bodies to learn from. It seems that criminals thought that having the body dissected after their deaths, was a fate worse than death itself and would only happen to the worst criminals around, making them rare to come across.

The Murder Act of 1752, was a law guideline that was written and consented to by the English Parliament. In it, the Act stated that any body of a murderer who was executed would be given to a local teaching hospital, where it was to be dissected to contribute to medical science. By doing this the parliament had hoped that fewer people would commit these crimes. Sadly, this was not the case.

This Act would be changed a few years after the Burke and Hare events.

Resurrectionist

Resurrectionist – *"A person who brings something to life or view again. a believer in resurrection. Also called resurrection man. a person who exhumes and steals dead bodies, especially for dissection; body snatcher".*

Dictionary.com

As the local medical schools lacked the resources of human cadavers, the poorer men in the City took it upon themselves to enter the graveyard, under the cover of darkness and find newly fresh graves. There they dug up the person and filled the hole back in and transported the corpse to one of the medical schools, where they would be paid extremally well for their efforts, by the Doctor. This term is now known as 'body snatching'.

It was not just the grave robbers who had a hand, in robbing the graves, other people informed the resurrectionists when someone was being buried, these people could be the gravediggers, undertakers or local officials, which would make a small profit by informing the body snatchers of a body.

Fortunately, for the resurrectionists, body snatching in the early 19th century was not a crime, as long as the people robbing the grave did not take any jewellery or clothing that belonged to the victims. If they were caught, they would more than likely be fined and the medical school would pay the fine. On occasional circumstances, if the robber were imprisoned the medical school would care for the family until that person was released for jail. In this case, it would be not the police that the resurrectionists were afraid of, it was the local people, who would riot and attack them. They were so disgusted that a person could unbury their loved ones from their resting place and sell them like they were a piece of meat.

There have been plenty of cases, in which the body snatchers were caught by a family member and a fight had been pursued. In Dublin, Ireland in 1828, a group of mourners approached a gang of resurrectionists, which made them leave as quickly as they arrived. The people in the cemetery decided to stick around to see if they would return to try and steal the body. In the meantime, more mourners joined the family and eventually, the body snatchers appeared again. This time the mourners were not forgiving and lynched the men. Firearms and other weapons were pulled out on either side and a fight was pursued. The outcome of this fight is unknown.

Five years later in 1832, in Northern Ireland, a group of resurrectionists were shot and killed for attempting to steal a corpse. Heading down to London in the same year, three men were stopped while transporting two deceased elderly men from their gravesite. A large crowd of people gathered around threatening the men and calling them murderers. It took forty police officers to move the resurrectionists into the police station.

Sometimes family members would take precautions into their own hands. Author Malcolm Archibald, wrote the book 'Bloody Scotland: Crime in 19th Century

Scotland', in it he claimed that a young boy from Dundee was buried and to prevent anyone from stealing his corpse, he buried his child with an exploding device inside the coffin.

Because of the increased popularity of this 'job', local people got to work to attempt to prevent the bodies from being disturbed. In the graveyards and cemeteries, brick watch towers were built, so that it enabled newly contracted watch guards to be placed on duty to prevent body snatching. Depending on the size of the cemetery, there would be up to three guards on duty during the night and each would walk around looking for suspicious activity.

More deterrents were erected in the graveyards, to give the family of their loved one's peace of mind, these include;

The building of Family Mausoleums – At first mausoleums were built by wealthy families. These were brick buildings, which usually had a trap door where a coffin would be taken underground and placed in a small chamber. The only problem with mausoleums was that if the building had a window, which many had, the body snatchers would just break it to gain entry. At the same time, a family member would stay inside the cold building, keeping watch of their family member for the first week or so. It is claimed that some of these family members who would keep watch, would end up being trapped inside and would become the next body to be placed in the mausoleum. To prevent this, a spare key would be hidden in the building, to enable an escape of the family watch guard.

Building of Mort Houses – Sometimes named the 'dead house'. Bodies of the recently deceased would be placed in mort houses until they had decomposed enough, that the resurrectionists could not sell them, then they would be buried in their usual form. These buildings were erected in cemeteries or nearby, so it was quick and easy to transport the deceased to their grave. In Scotland and Northern England, there were 31 mort houses available to use.

If the winter was particularly cold, the ground would be frozen, making it harder to dig a grave. During these times, the bodies would have to be placed into a mort house, until the ground was soft enough to dig.

Mortsafes – Mortsafes were produced in the 19th century to prevent the body snatchers from getting anywhere near the coffin. It consisted of a metal or iron frame that was situated on top of the grave. The mortsafes were particularly common in Scotland and some can be still seen today. The downside of having a mortsafe is that it was only the rich that could afford one to be made. If you could not afford one, family members would take it in turn, to sit at the gravesite to watch for resurrectionists, until it was deemed that the body had been in the ground long enough to not be needed by the anatomists.

Production of Coffin Collars – A coffin collar was a piece of metal that was fixed onto the wood. The metal was placed around a corpse's neck and bolted down to the coffin that the deceased was lying in. the coffin collars came into use around the 1820s in Scotland, to make it harder for the resurrectionists to steal a body. This was not as expensive as the mortsafes, but would still come at a cost. Again, mostly wealthy families could only afford the determents that prevented the resurrectionists from extracting the dead from their graves.

An example of the lengths people went to, to prevent grave robbing

How Resurrectionists would work

Resurrectionists would work in a small gang and would work during the night. As they would a new dug grave, each member would help to dig one side of the grave, all the way down to the coffin, to prevent much noise coming from the cemetery it is claimed that a sack or canvas of some sort would be placed over the top. As they got to the coffin, the body snatchers would open the coffin lid and slip the corpse out. The corpse would be undressed and any jewellery would be taken off and left in the now empty coffin. The body would then be placed in a sac and carried to the local Anatomist, where they would receive up to £10, depending on the time of year and how fresh the corpse was. The whole process of digging and filling the grave back up would have taken around half an hour.

It is unknown how many bodies were taken from their resting places in the 19th century. It was possible that thousands of bodies were stolen each year. Could it be that everyone who was buried in the 18th and early 19th century without any precautions was still lying in their coffin or were they all stolen? Unfortunately, we will never know.

THE PEOPLE

William Burke

William Burke was born in Urney in County Tyrone in 1792, which is situated in Northern Ireland. Burke was one of two children for his father Neil Burke and his mother with the possible maiden name of Docherty. His brother Constantine Burke was two years older than William, born in 1790.

William Burke – Dailyrecord.co.uk

After a comfortable early upbringing. William spent a lot of time with a Presbyterian teacher, learning how to read and write, something that lower-class people did not know how to do in this era. This would come in handy by the end of his life when he wrote another confession while incarcerated in his jail cell.

William Burke joined the Irish military by the age of 19 in 1811, where it is claimed that he worked as a manservant to an Officer. It is stated that William Burke served in the Donegal Militia for seven years. It was during this time that he met his future wife, Margaret Coleman, near to where he was based in Ballina.

Margaret Coleman was born in Ballina, County Mayo in Northern Ireland in 1794. She was two years younger than William. The couple married in County Mayo; however, I cannot find any actual proof of this. It is stated that Margaret and William Burke had at least two children together. Author Dudley-Owens claimed that William and Margaret may have married due to her falling pregnant early on in their relationship. This pregnancy did not convince William to leave his job and it is possible that while William was in the military, his wife Margaret was living with her father and child.

Around 1818, William Burke left the military and one of the stories is that he was expected to receive some land of his father-in-law, when this did not happen the men began to argue. During this time, it was possible that Margaret was pregnant again and being fed up with his life outside the Army, William Burke decided to pack up his belongings and flee to Scotland for a new start, leaving his wife and children behind. Whether they wanted to go across with him or not is unknown. The family seemed to be heavily involved in religion and immigrating to another country at the time was like losing their faith and was shunned upon. This could be the reason why Margaret did not leave Ireland with her husband.

By now, William's brother Constantine had already left Ireland and was living in Edinburgh. He found himself a job working in the Police station and had a fairly comfortable life, living in a room with his wife Elizabeth and their three children.

William Burke left Ireland and sailed over to Scotland. There he settled down in Maddiston, Falkirk, where he found a job working on the build of the Union Canal as a Navvy.

NAVVY – *"A Navvy is a person who is employed to do hard physical work, for example building roads or canals".*

Collinsdictionary.com

On a typical Sunday is was not unusual to see William Burke walking around holding a bible. He attended Church regularly until he decided to settle down with a woman named Helen McDougal, but she preferred to be called Nelly for short. Knowing that William was already married, he was encouraged to leave Helen by the church and go back to Ireland to be with his family. It seems that William was the happiest that he had been in a long time and refused to do what the Church wanted him to. It was from this refusal that the church excommunicated him and he was left basically without religion and a safe haven.

William Burke and Helen MacDougal did not marry but they lived as a common-law husband and wife. They stayed in Maddiston until the Union Canal was finished in 1822, living happily and at peace. They often spoke of what they were going to do when the work was complete on the canal. He thought about moving further down Scotland and he was going to open a cobbler business.

It is unknown exactly what William and Helen did when the work was completed and what we do know is sparse. For a while, the couple moved down to Peebles in Southern Scotland but would spend the summer harvesting. Around 1827, William had met a woman named Margaret Logue. It is possible that he knew Margaret before this date as they both came from Ireland. Margaret ran a lodging house in West Port of Edinburgh and invited William and Helen to come to stay at her place. She even provided him space in the stables, where he could open a cobbler shop. Getting along rather well with Margaret the couple agreed to give Edinburgh a try and packed up the little belongings that they had and make their way into the city.

After arriving in Edinburgh, the couple moved to Log's Lodging House in Tanners Close, West Port around November 1827.

While living at the lodging house William Burke became a Hawker. He would buy or find old shoes and fix them up and then he would send Helen out onto the small streets selling the shoes and some second and third-hand clothes to the locals. It was not long before Burke realised that the people, he was selling the clothes to did not have much money. This left him not making much profit and they struggled to pay their rent, as he had produced a drinking habit as well as taking opium on a regular basis. Around this time William Burke was claimed to have earned one pound or more each week, which is a lot more than the other people that lived around him.

William Burke was still a religious man. It seemed that when he was excommunicated, he decided to change his religion from Catholicism. He regularly attended religious meetings at the Grassmarket with his fellow Presbyterian's.

Maddiston, Falkirk

The town of Maddiston was originally named Muiravonside in a charter as early as 1424. The town itself is around five miles away from the centre of Falkirk, sitting to the east. However, it seems that a named change was accepted by the locals and by Timothy Point's map of the area between 1583 and 1596, the town was known as Madistoun.

Around 1424, the local church named Muiravonside Parish Church was erected near Haining Castle. This allowed the locals of the villages that were situated close by to have a place of worship. During the week, the children from the areas would attend some sort of schooling in the building, however, most children would only be educated for a couple of years before going out to work.

The Old Polmont Parish Church

The present building that you can see today was built in 1806 by a man named George Hays and it is more than likely that William Burke had worshipped there. Around this time, it was found out that there was indeed another church on this site before the present building, which stood in what is now the Kirkyard (Churchyard).

By the 1930s the first school at Muiravonside was built, meaning the children had their own building which was dedicated to their education.

In 1955, the church was forced to be refurnished due to its condition and woodworm. The seating positions were changed and a new pulpit and chancel were added.

Around this time, the name had changed once again to Maddiston. The village was popular for stone quarrying. The local quarries were located at the back of Lawson Place, Cairnymount Avenue area, Manualrigg, then later at Haining, as well as the many smaller quarries dotted around the villages.

At the start of the twentieth-century coal had been found beneath the ground. This led to The Carron Mining Company operating its services in Maddiston. It also brought in many more jobs for the locals. Unfortunately, many coal pits were closed before 1930, however, some independent companies carried on working until the 1960s. The last site to close in the 1960s is now the Polmont Golf Club.

Helen MacDougal

Not much is known about Helen MacDougal. Variations of her surname are spelt M'Dougal (which is the old spelling), McDougal or MacDougall.

Author Owen Dudley Edwards claimed that Helen MacDougal came from Redding near Falkirk, however, I cannot pinpoint a birth certificate for her. She was probably born between 1870 and 1890.

Helen MacDougal – Nationalgalleries.org

Edwards, also claimed that MacDougal was probably not her surname. He claimed that she once settled with a man and lived as his common wife, without them getting married. It was here that she took on his surname MacDougal.

"It is certain that Helen McDougal (or rather Dougal, for that is her proper name), never was married: she absconded from home with a married man of the name of M'Dougal, long before she knew Burke, and had two children by him: he is the father of Gray's wife".

Burke and Hare – William Roughead (1921)

According to the Stentmaister family, in their research in July 2014, they narrowed Helen MacDougall down to two people. One of them being a woman named Helen Galloway. Galloway was born to parents William Galloway and Jean Easton on the 24th of December 1794. This makes Helen Galloway slightly more likely to be Helen MacDougal as she would indeed have been 33-year-old when she was interviewed by Sherriff Tait, which is the same age as MacDougal claimed to be.

Looking into Helen Galloway there is no record of her death or whereabouts during her life.

We know from Burke's confessions that he met Helen in or near Maddiston, where they set up home together. She may have worked as a prostitute around this time. However, this is hearsay and we cannot say that this was definite.

Around this time that William Burke and Helen began living together, her first common-law husband MacDougall had died and she was living with another unknown man but chose William Burke over him.

Also in the confession, William Burke stated that he took Helen back to the Falkirk area to stay with family for a few weeks during 1828 and that it was a yearly routine to watch a parade.

Unfortunately, we do not know anymore.

William Hare

William Hare's life was harder to track down than William Burke's and not much is known about him, especially his early childhood. Hare was probably born in County Londonderry in Ireland. One biographer stated that he was born between the years 1792 and 1804 in County, Armagh, Northern Ireland.

William Hare - scotclans.com

It is claimed that William Hare worked as an agricultural labourer before moving to Scotland, however, he was unmarried and did not have any children.

According to the book 'Old and New Edinburgh' written by James Grant, William Hare at one point was working in Hopetoun in South Queensferry, Scotland. There it is claimed that he worked at the Port as a Labourer. His main job was to load and unload the boats that docked in the area.

Like Burke, William Hare managed to get a job with the Canal Union in 1818, which at the time the union was making the Canal systems throughout Britain. If William Hare was born in 1804, it would have made him approximately 14 years old, when he left home, travelled to Scotland and found a job. Even for this era, it does not make sense. Either he was born in Scotland or he was older than other researchers have thought and in the police document, his age must have been written incorrectly.

When there was no more work left, Hare moved to Edinburgh and rented a room in Logs Lodging in Tanner's Close at the West Port in Edinburgh. The lodging house was run by a woman named Margaret Laird, who married a man with the surname of Logue or Loag. William Hare began staying in the lodging house after the work had finished on the canal. William Hare found a job as a coal man's assistant, so he could pay his landlords; Logue and Margaret Laird their rent.

He soon found himself in an affair with Margaret, which caught her husbands' attention. William Hare was swiftly kicked out of the house, only to return after his death in 1826 and he married Margaret at Saint Cuthbert's Church, Edinburgh, Midlothian, on the 16th of August 1826 and ran the lodging house with her.

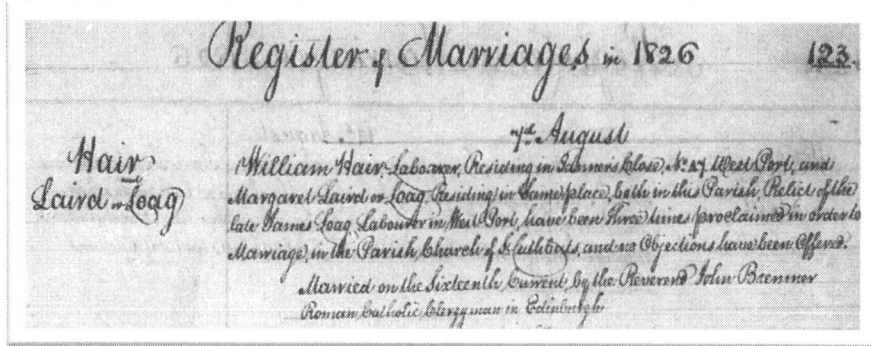

Old Parish Marriage Register 1826

It is claimed that during 1827 William Hare had sent his wife Margaret to Penicuik to work on the Harvest. It is here that she met William Burke and his partner Helen MacDougal, perhaps for the first time. It was Margaret who convinced her new friends to come to Edinburgh and stay at the lodging house. The friends decided to see what the city was like and they travelled back to Edinburgh after the harvest season had finished and William Burke and his common-law wife moved into their guest house on Tanners Close.

However, is it feasible that Burke and Hare did not know each other until this time? They lived nearby one another and they both worked for the Union Canal near Falkirk.

From this date the two couples were inseparable.

St Cuthbert's Parish Church, Edinburgh

St Cuthbert's church is situated on the outer walls of Edinburgh's old town. When the first church was being built during the reign of the Scottish King David I (1124 – 1153). The name of St Cuthbert came from the Anglo-Saxon Saint, which lived in Scotland during the 600's. Cuthbert became a Monk after spotting an apparition or had a vision.

During the next few hundred years, the church was burnt down or destroyed at least twice, due to the war between the Scottish and the English. The first time was in 1385 when King Richard II, decided to lead his army north into Scotland and burned Holyrood Palace and Edinburgh. The second time happened in 1544 when the Earl of

L.A Mackay

Hertford was sent by King Henry VIII to enforce marriage between Mary, Queen of Scots and Henry's son, Edward. Henry wanted his son to marry the Queen of Scotland, so that the Tudors could take over the throne of Scotland, giving England more power. The marriage was refused and this left the English angry. They decided to take their revenge and destroyed the Border Abbeys, Holyrood and Edinburgh, which included St Cuthbert's leaving it was severe damage.

In 1650 Oliver Cromwell (rule 1653 – 1658) and his army won the Scots at the Battle of Dunbar. Cromwell and his people decided to make St Cuthbert's their temporary home and destroyed the interior. The roof of the building was also destroyed by gunshots, cannons and muskets.

Thirty-nine years after Oliver Cromwell's visit to the church, St Cuthbert's was destroyed again, this time in the Glorious Revolution in 1689. The building was damaged by canon fire

By the 1700s the church had been run down into the ground and a new church was designed to be built in place of the old church. While building, it is claimed that some of the relics of St Cuthbert had been excavated, which included an urn, human bones and a leaden coffin. It is said that the urn had a fragrance that smelt sweet, when the urn was open a human heart that had not been embalmed was found sitting in the pot. It was found out that these items may have belonged to a man from the crusades who passed away while on his travels to the Holy Land. After this man's death, his remains were taken back home to be buried.

During the Jacobite rebellion at the beginning of the 18th century, the Jacobite's used St Cuthbert's as their station.

In the middle of the 1770s, St Cuthbert's was rebuilt and their new church was opened on the 11th of July 1775. Another rebuilding took place in the 19th century and was opened on the 11th of July 1894. This is the church that you can see today.

Margaret Laird

Margaret Laird was the daughter of William Laird and an unknown mother who were originally from Raphoe, County Donegal in Ireland. She was born in 1785 in perhaps Glasgow, Scotland or she moved to Scotland later on in life.

Unfortunately, nothing is known about Margaret's early life.

Old Parish Marriage Register 1814

By 1814, Margaret was living in Edinburgh, Scotland. She married a man named James Logue or Loag, in Canongate on the 19th of October 1814. In the church document it states;

"19th October 1814
Loag – James Loag, Labourer. No 27 High Street, Canongate, 2nd
Marry and Margaret Laird in Glasgow, Daughter of late William
Laird, Labourer, parish of Raphoe, in Ireland, gave up their names
for marriage.
Certified by John Monro, Weaver, Nethery Street, Edin, and
Rodrick McDonald, Labourer, Midcommon Close, Canongate".
Canongate Old Parish Marriage Register

It is probable that Margaret and James moved into number 27 High Street until they brought a lodging house in Tanner Close, West Port, where they would open their house up to destitute people of the area.

Margaret Laird's house on Canongate was situated near here

In 1825, Margaret gave birth to a son on the 9th of June. It is unknown what the child was named. Unfortunately, their baby would only live for twenty days and passed away on the 29th of June that year.

It was around this time that William Hare made his way to Edinburgh and stayed with Margaret and James Loag. After staying with the couple for a while, it became clear to James that Margaret may be sleeping with the custom. After a heated discussion, William Hare packed up his belongings and left Log's Lodging house and moved elsewhere.

Although we do not know, it seemed that things went back to normal in the lodging house, however, it is possible that Margaret was still seeing William Hare.

Margaret's husband James Loag passed away unexpectedly on the 2nd of February 1826 at their home. He was 45 years old. This can document can be found in the Old Parish Death Register of St Cuthbert's. His passing left Margaret with a lodging house to run herself and it was not long until William Hare moved back.

Showing James Loag's death - Old Parish Death Register 1826

Some authors theorised that James Loag would have been William Hare's first victim. We do not think this is possible because when the crimes got going, Burke and Hare killed the people because they wanted to sell their bodies to the local teaching surgeon. If this was the case and Loag was indeed Hare's victim, his death was recorded and he was buried, meaning this could not be a profit killing.

On the 7th of August 1826, six months after her husband's passing, Margaret Laird married William Hare at St Cuthbert's Church in Edinburgh. The parish records states;

"Register of Marriage in 1826
7th August
Hair & Laird or Loag *– William Hair, Labourer, Residing in Tanner's Close, No 47 West Port and Margaret Laird or Loag, residing in same place, both in this parish relic of the late James Loag, Labourer, in West Port have been three times proclaimed in order to marriage in the parish church of St Cuthbert's and no objections has been offered.*
Married on the sixteenth current by the Reverend John Bremmer, Roman Catholic Clergyman in Edinburgh".
St Cuthbert's Parish Marriage Register

Although married to William Hare, Margaret's surname would always be known as Laird or Log (rather than Loag).

It seems that the Hare's were either struggling for money or they were greedy and liked a lot of money. In the summer of 1827, Margaret Laird headed west for the harvest and it is here that she met William Burke and his partner Helen MacDougal. That season, they had fun getting to know one another and Margaret asked William Hare and Helen McDougal to move into her lodging house in Edinburgh. The couple were already thinking about their plans on what to do next, but somehow Margaret managed to convince them to try living in the city for a while. This was not all kindness and sweethearts, as Margaret will have two extra customers and more money in her pocket. By the end of the season, all three travelled back to Edinburgh, where William Burke was introduced to Margaret's husband William Hare.

Tanner's Close, West Port

Tanner's Close was situated in West Port of Edinburgh, just a short walk from the famous Grassmarket area. In Burke and Hare's time, the area was occupied by some of the poorest people in the city.

The area was named West Port because it was the only way out of Edinburgh in the western direction. Before you entered West Port, there was a huge gate and wall, which allowed people in and out of the area. This would come to be known as the Flodden Wall.

The Flodden Wall is a part of the city walls which surrounded the old town of Edinburgh. It was erected in the 1500s after the Scots were defeated by the English at the battle of Flodden. These walls which included King's Wall and Telfer Wall were made to be approximately twenty-four feet tall and nearly four feet thick. It was made as a defence mechanism for the city and only had half a dozen openings to get in and out of the city.

Flodden Wall in Greyfriars Kirk

The openings to the Flodden Wall were used to display the head and limbs of criminals as a warning to all that came and went from the old city.

Most of the City's Walls were destroyed by the 1800s, however, there are a few places that you can still see the wall or where the wall was in place in the city.

Log's Lodging House was located through a small, narrow and dirty close which led from the north side of the street of West Port. This appears to be the same name today. Most of the description of the house was written by George MacGregor in 1884. In it, he states that when you entered the close, you had to walk down a few steps into an alleyway where the house was situated. The building was ground floor level and was consisted of three apartments, where if you were to walk down the close, you would see the Hare's front door. A sign stating 'Beds to let' was seen outside of the building.

Part of Tanners Close can be still seen today

The house looked small from the outside but was quite a size when you stepped in with a stable at the end of the close. Inside the house contained seven beds. The first room was fully furnished with an open fire. Today we would say it was a kitchen, where guests and friends would sit around drinking and making good conversation. When you entered the two bedrooms inside the house, the beds were made from fir trees with a mattress made from straw. The sheets on the bed were grey with an added brown blanket for warmth from the Scottish weather.

After the crimes were discovered, Log's Lodging House was raided. It is unknown if the house was occupied by anyone else. It is known that the houses in Tanner's Close began to crumble due to their ag and lack of repairs.

In the 1893 Ordnance Survey map, Log's Lodging House was still listed as a building in the area. This would only last for a few more years, before the city council tore down the slums of Edinburgh in 1902, taking the infamous house with it. Where Tanner's close was situated is now an office block, named Argyle House.

THE UNION CANAL

It was a big challenge to get items delivered in and out of the city of Edinburgh before the 19th century. One item that the city lacked was coal. A limited supply would reach the city by boat but this was not enough for the over-crowding situation and it was very expensive. Many jobs such as blacksmiths and bakeries needed a coal fire to be able to produce their products.

In the 1790s plans were set in motion for Scotland to have several canals built, so that small boats would be able to deliver items on land and to the city. One of these plans was for the Union Canal.

Another twenty-one years would pass before anything was done with these plans, as the Scots were involved in the Napoleonic War between 1800 and 1803 and finding the money to fund the canal was proving to be difficult.

The plan was for the Union Canal to begin at Falkirk and make its way to Edinburgh via Polmont, Linlithgow, Winchburgh, Broxburry, Ratho and into Edinburgh. The length would be thirty-one miles and it would follow the natural contours of the land.

An engineer named Hugh Bourd looked at the plans and showed where the Union Canal could join the Forth and Clyde Canal through a series of locks, making the canal system to be able to reach further afield.

The Union Canal would be built at one level, as this would make it cheaper to do and it would also make the boats travel faster in and out of the city.

Work began on the Union Canal during March 1818 and would last four years, ending in 1822. Many Irish men came over to Scotland, to build the canal and they would stay nearby, building business for the local lodging house and shops. After the canal was complete, many Irish decided to stay in Scotland and find work elsewhere.

For a relatively short period of time, the canal was a success. Cheaper coal was brought into the city via boats and everyone was happy. The local people of Edinburgh were able to venture out of the city on day trips on canal boats, which was inexpensive.

The Union Canal 2021

Unfortunately, twenty years later in 1842, a railway system between Glasgow and Edinburgh was opened. This was to be able to transport goods even quicker and also included passenger services. This put the end to the use of the canals and by 1848 work has ceased on them completely.

In the early 20th century, it was decided that the canal was a useless space and was filled in, giving more land for local housing. The official closing date for the canal was in 1965, but the usage had stopped well before then.

L.A Mackay

However, with the arrival of the millennium, the local councils voted to have the canal dug out again, spending £8.2 million on the project. At the time this was the largest canal restoration project seen in the United Kingdom. As well as this, the Falkirk wheel was added. The canal was re-opened in 2002.

The canal is used for leisure purposes now, with small barges sailing in the water, and walkers and cyclists ride on the path beside it.

A NEW LIFE

In August 1827, William Burke and Helen MacDougal arrived in Edinburgh with Margaret Laird. Margaret brought the couple back to her home in Tanner's Court and they were quickly introduced to William Hare and pretty soon the foursome got on well. When they were not working, the two couples spent a lot of time together.

William Burke set up a cobbler shop in the stable of the house and Helen MacDougal would go out on the streets to sell the items that he sold as well as second-hand clothes, that came into their possession. After having several different jobs such as labourer or baker, William Burke was taught how to fix shoes while working on the Union Canal.

Although the city was busier than what William Burke was used to, he felt right at home in the West Port. He was not the only family member who was living in Edinburgh at that time. His brother Constantine Burke, was living with his wife and three children in Gibb's Close on Canongate. It was around a twenty-minute walk.

Constantine arrived in Edinburgh before William Burke. He lived with his wife Elizabeth (nee. Graham) and their three children. A daughter named Elizabeth and two sons named Richard and William. To make ends meet, Constantine as a scavenger worked for the Police in Edinburgh and he left his wife at home to look after the house.

SCAVENGER – *"Scavengers were employed by the police to clean up the streets, much like a janitor or binman would do today".*
Sheila Cameron Oliver, MA, (1995)

William Burke, William Hare and their partners had only known each other for a short time. They would spend most of their days together drinking whisky and talking about life in Ireland. They would dance and sing until the early hours of the morning. Other researchers claimed that when the men were sober, they were cheerful especially William Burke, but after they supplied themselves with plenty of alcohol, their personalities changed.

It seems like at the beginning of life in Edinburgh, William Burke and Helen McDougal struggled to make ends meet. This would all change in December 1827.

DR ROBERT KNOX

Robert Knox was born on the 4th of September 1791 in Edinburgh, Scotland to parents Robert Knox and Mary Scherer. At the time of his birth, Knox had seven older siblings.

When Robert Knox turned 19 years old, he began learning at the University of Edinburgh. He knew what he wanted to do with his life from an early age when he suffered smallpox. Robert Knox wanted to become a doctor.

After graduating from university in 1814, Knox moved down to London where he began to work for St Bartholomew's Hospital for a year. From there he was sent to Belgium where he attended to the wounded at the Battle of Waterloo. In his spare time, we would begin to look for a cure for syphilis.

In 1817, Robert Knox joined the 72nd Highlanders and travelled to South Africa with them. He later claimed to have found this very boring because his duties were light and infrequent. He left the army after they sent him home for fighting with an ex-naval officer after the officer challenged him to a duel. Knox refused to fight the man, but the officer whipped him in front of all the men, so Knox cut his arm. He lost his promotion and his job at the same time. Returning to the United Kingdom during the Christmas period of 1820.

After ten months, Robert Knox was bored again and decided to travel to Paris, France. It is here that he studied anatomy. After this, he returned home to Edinburgh.

In December 1823, Knox was elected to join the Royal Society of Edinburgh. It was a group to help improve the advances of medical science and only the best professors joined the establishment. It was around this time that he used animals to write

L.A Mackay

zoological papers.

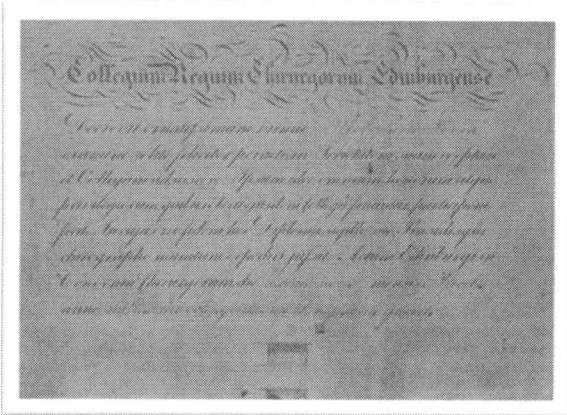

Robert Knox's diploma

The following year Robert Knox settled down and married a woman named Susan. The wedding took place in secret and they lived apart with Knox living at 4 Newington Place and Susan living at Lilliput Cottage in Leith. Here she gave birth to seven of his children. Unfortunately, only two of the children lived to adulthood.

Robert Knox opened his theatre in Edinburgh which challenged the 'boring' Alexander Monro. His lessons had become increasingly popular with his students and other visitors. He became partners with Dr John Barclay at the school and it went from strength to strength. He had a house at 10 Surgeons Square which was situated in High School Yards, where his surgical school was located, which was situated close to the building that we now know as Old Surgeons Hall.

High School Yards 2021 (behind me is the Old High School Building)

It seems that before Burke and Hare turned up at his door of 10 Surgeons Square, Dr Robert Knox had already been buying corpses from resurrectionists to help his lectures, as he promised a fresh body per day. This was usually because, at the time, the Doctors were only receiving a few corpses a year.

High School Yards

Nearly 400 years before our story, begins the known history of High School Yards. The land was founded by King Alexander II in 1230 and a monastery was built upon the site, which was known as Blackfriars. The monastery had a few acres of land which surrounded it, which some of it was made into a beautiful garden named the Dominican Gardens. After passing the garden, there was another church named St Mary in the Field, which was surrounded by houses, one of the named 'old provost's house'. It was at this house on the 10th of February 1567, that Mary Queen of Scots husband and father to her son James, a man named Lord Henry Stewart Darnley was staying, while he recovered from smallpox.

Murder

During Lord Darnley's stay at the old provost house, his wife Mary visited him. She brought him new bedding to make him feel more comfortable during his stay. It was agreed between the couple that he would stay there until he was fully recovered so that the illness did not pass on to their eight-month-old son James, who was next in line for the Scottish throne.

In the late hours of the 9th and the early hours of the 10th of February, Mary Queen of Scots was attending a wedding party at Holyrood Palace, while Lord Darnley was attempting to keep himself occupied. Eventually, Lord Darnley decided to retire to bed for the night. From this point on we do not know any more about the story.

During the early hours, an explosion erupted from the old provost house. Several witnesses and neighbours who had been awoken by the noise rushed into the street. Upon investigation, they found Lord Dudley's half-naked deceased body in the garden, alongside one of his male servants. Some people who inspected the two corpses blamed their deaths on not the explosion but strangulation.

Eventually, suspicion fell onto his wife Mary and the Earl of Bothwell, who would marry three months after Lord Darnley's death. This was the start of Mary Queen of Scot's downfall.

Riot

In 1558, nine years before Lord Darnley's death, the Blackfriars monastery had serious damage of its own. A Scottish minister named John Knox declared to his people that he had changed from being a catholic to a protestant. This was at a time where more of Europe were preaching Catholicism and a change of religion was more or less unheard of in Scotland. However, for England, it was a different matter. King Henry VIII had inherited the title of King from his father King Henry VII after his older brother Arthur passed away shortly after his wedding day. King Henry VIII, married Catherine of Aragon and for 24 years, their marriage continued. However, there was a huge problem for Henry. He desperately needed a male heir to continue to Tudor line of succession, but Catherine had several children that resulted in premature deaths or miscarriages. By now, a woman named Anne Boleyn had caught Henry's attention, however, being with her would come at a cost.

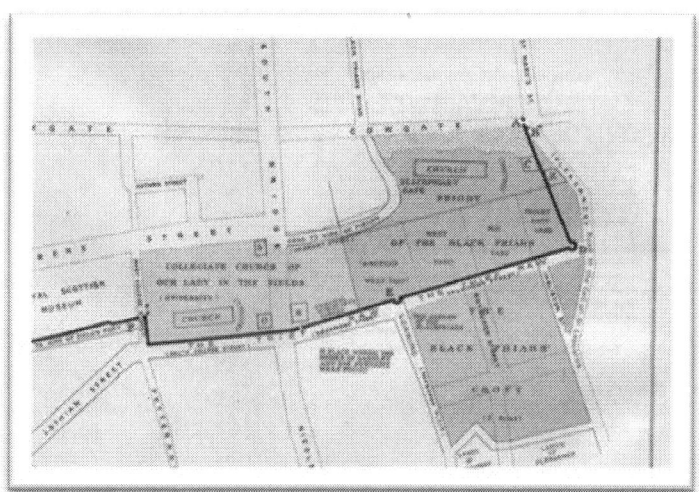

Blackfriars Monastery - scotland.op.org

Anne refused to have anything to do with Henry until he married her, making her Queen of England. When Henry approached the head of the Catholic church, the Pope did not agree to his request. Henry although angry with the church, decided to take action and make his own church, where he was head and could do whatever, he liked. This is when the Church of England was formed. To add to this matter, Henry got revenge on the Catholic church when he decided to shut down all the monasteries and ordered his men to take everything that could get them money. Even the lead from the roof was removed.

For a time, Knox moved to England, however, when he arrived back in Scotland, he travelled around East Lothian where he taught people about the reformation. This seemed to have un-nerved some of the biggest Catholic followers, while some Scots decided to follow his ways and reverted to his beliefs.

John Knox continued to travel around Scotland and ended up being in Exile in England, where he was allowed to preach for the Church of England.

In July 1553, John Knox's now settled life over turned when Queen Mary I was crowned the Queen of England. Mary was a strict Catholic and declared that England would be a catholic country again. By the January of the following years, John Knox had fled to France, ending up in Geneva.

The English already had their reformation, when King Henry VIII set up his religion, now by 1559, it was the Scottish turn, to rebel against Catholicism. Like the English, they did not fight quietly. A group of rebels decided to hit the Catholics right where it hurts and chose to go after the friars. They had a belief that if they destroyed the monasteries, the friars would lose their homes and hopefully their faith.

By May of that year, the group travelled to Perth, where they destroyed Greyfriars monastery. They stole everything that they would even the windows and doors. The rebels then made their way to Edinburgh, where they did the same to Blackfriars. After this rebellion, there was nothing left. The friars ran out, some left Edinburgh and the others stayed with their catholic friends. Even Mary Queen of Scots cared for two of the friars from Blackfriars. The only thing that was left of the monastery was a bunch of ruins, the cemetery and the gardens.

The Buildings

High School of Edinburgh

Over the years, High School Yards has changed a lot. The area got its name when the High School of Edinburgh was built by Alexander Laing in 1777, at the cost of £4000. Two of the most famous pupils of the school was Sir Walter Scott (Author and Poet) and James Pillans (inventor of the chalkboard and coloured chalk).

As the population in Edinburgh increased and the New Town was made, it became apparent that the building was not large enough to support all the students.

A new School below Carlton Hill was erected in 1829. They named this school the Royal High School, which still stands to the present day (2021). With pupils now preferring a more modern school, the High School of Edinburgh was no longer needed and was taken over by the University of Edinburgh in 1832. The building was now used as a surgical hospital and it's here that the anatomy classes were performed by the university professors.

As the population was still on the increase and the need for medical care was needed more than ever, the surgical hospital was made to be an extension for the Royal Edinburgh Hospital, which was located nearby. The main building of the hospital was designed now just for cases, while the extension (surgical hospital) was to carry out operations and post mortems.

L.A Mackay

The New Royal Infirmary

By 1852, the old hospital was falling into disrepair, so a plan was put together for another hospital to be built in its place. Unfortunately, if you visit surgeons square today, there is no sign of the old hospital, except for the gate posts as they enter the grounds.

The building that replaced the infirmary would be used as a hospital for infectious diseases. This only lasted for a short time. It was demolished in 1884, where brand new buildings were built in place. This included a local swimming pool and a school for young children.

The New Surgical Hospital

In the middle of the 1800's a man named David Bryce designed and built a new hospital. The reason for this new built was as an extension due to the increase of need.

As time went on and a new hospital was made elsewhere, what to do with the old buildings was unknown. In 1906 Andrew Carnegie opened the Department of Natural Philosophy on the site of the New Surgical Infirmary. The building remained this way for seventy years before the Departments of Physics and Meteorology moved in, in 1976. This area still occupies the building as of the present year (2021).

Houses in Surgeon's Square

Surgeon's Square is situated behind the old infirmary and school, it held many private houses, which belonged to Doctors and Surgeons. One of these houses (10 Surgeon's Square) was owned by Dr Robert Knox, who used this location to teach his anatomy classes to his students and was watched by the paying public.

Unfortunately, over the years, the houses in Surgeons Square have disappeared and have been replaced by other buildings, however, one still exists and can show us, what the houses in the area would have looked like. The building is known as Chisholm House.

Chisholm House was built in 1764 and was named after George Chisholm, who was the first Geography lecturer at the University. It is a tall building with four floors plus a basement.

The Old Surgeons Hall

on the south side of Surgeons Square lays the old surgeons hall. The hall was occupied by the local surgeons in 1697 and remained that way until 1832. A plaque which still stands outside the building states;

"1697, The Edinburgh surgeons moved from their former meeting place in Dickson's Close to this building. Here they conducted their business until they moved to the present ROYAL COLLEGE OF SURGEONS in Nicholson Street in 1832".

In more recent years, the dental side of the university took over the occupancy of the building, then it became the social science school in 1995. Today the building is linked to the Study of Science, Technology and Innovation.

THE CRIMES

Burke and Hare committed around sixteen crimes; however, we do not know the details of every single one of these murders and what we do know are taken from newspaper accounts, broadsides, confessions and word of mouth. Some of these may be false but it is also possible that more murders were committed.

A retired man named Donald (surname unknown) lived at Tanners Close with the couples in 1927 and due to his ill health, he died unexpectedly of Dropsy on the 27th or 29th of November 1827. Donald received a regular pension four times a year and would pay his board when he received the money. It turned out that this money should have been given to him a few weeks after his death. William Hare was angry that Donald died so near to the pension because he owed the Hares £4 and now, they were out of pocket.

Dropsy – *"Edema, called dropsy long ago, is swelling caused by fluid retention. This condition usually occurs in your feet, legs, or ankles. However, it can also occur in your hands, your face, or any other part of the body".*

Healthline.com

William Hare went through the usual channels and managed to get a cheap coffin which was provided by the local undertaker, to lay Donald's body in before his quick pauper burial. Still reeling with the thought of not getting the rent he was owed, William Hare attempted to think of ways that he could recover his loss.

It is unknown which William thought of the idea to steal Donald's body and take it to the anatomists to sell, many documentaries and researchers claimed that it was

William Hare's idea and depicted that William Burke was not keen on the plan. Hare managed to talk William Burke round and they soon found themselves, taking the nails out of the coffin and extracting Donald from his resting place. The men knew that if an empty box was picked up by the undertaker, it would have been pretty obvious that the body was not in the wooden box, so they headed to the back of Tanners Court, where they knew that a pile of bark was sitting for the fire and by handfuls, they carried the bark into the house, where they began to fill up the empty coffin. When the coffin came to a decent weight, the men placed a sheet that was originally covering Donald's body over the top of the bark, in hope that some of the odour would make it smell like a person was inside, then the two men nailed the lid closed again. Not long after this, the undertaker came to collect the body for the burial.

Burke and Hare knew that the local anatomists were only allowed a few bodies a year to teach their students and knew that men would go into graveyards and dig up the recently deceased to sell them on to the Doctors. They decided to walk down to the medical school to find a willing participant to claim the body. As they approached the area, they spoke to a student, who told the men to visit a man named Dr Knox and pointed him in the direction of 10 Surgeon's Square.

When they arrived at the door, they did not know what to expect. They spoke to one of Dr Knox's assistants and he told the men to come back with the body after dark and to make sure that no one should see them and that is what they did.

The men placed Donald's body in a sac and carried it to 10 Surgeons Square. Again, the assistant answered the door and brought the men and the body inside. William Burke and William Hare were asked to get the body out and lay it on the table to be looked at. When asked how the men had come across the body, the men came up with an excuse and claimed that their landlord wanted rid of the body because it was bad for business. Not challenging the men on this story, the assistant gave Burke and Hare £7 and 10 shillings for their trouble. In today's money, they would have received a little over £430.

Upon leaving the building Dr Knox's assistant commented that if they came across any more bodies, he would be happy to accept them in return for a great sum of money. This left the men with an idea.

At last William Hare calmed down from his rage, he had got his back payment as the money was split. Hare received £4 and 5 Shillings and Burke got a tidy sum of £3 and 5 shillings. Not bad for a day's work!

The men were thinking about what the assistant said and they thought that it was easy money to earn. Burke and Hare thought about taking in lodgers which were close to death so that they would wait for them to pass away and sell their bodies. This proved in taking too much time and they were not getting anywhere.

It is unknown whose body them sold next, due to the conflicting confessions of both William Burke and William Hare. Unfortunately, William Hare's confession has been lost to history and a man named Walter Scott was the only person to read both confessions. He took it upon himself to believe Hare's events and claimed that Abigail Simpson was the next and first 'victim' of Burke and Hare. However, I feel that Joseph is next in line, as it makes more sense to the build-up of murders.

In December 1827, a man named Joseph, who was said to have worked as a miller fell ill in Tanner's Court. Joseph was living in the guest house at the time. In one of Burke's confessions towards the end of his life, he claimed that Joseph worked at Falkirk in the Ironworks and was not an agricultural labourer at all.

William Burke and William Hare, frequently checked on the man, hoping that they would walk into the room to find him dead. However, this was not the case and poor Joseph continued to battle on through his illness.

Burke and Hare were far too impatient to see if Hare's lodger would die of natural causes and Hare took it upon himself to give him a little push in the right direction. The men decided to ply Joseph with as much whisky as he could take in hope that it would kill him or he would pass out and be less defensive. Eventually, Joseph died fall to sleep and that is when William Hare, pounced on the unsuspected man and attempted to smother him, but blocking his nose and keeping his mouth closed. Joseph fought back and Hare called on Burke to pin him down to make him useless and after a few minutes, Joseph had died.

Like before they waited until dark and took his freshly deceased body to 10 Surgeons Square to see Dr Knox, where they sold his body for £10.

Next was a lady named Abigail Simpson, who was a salt seller on the streets of Edinburgh and in the local areas. Abigail Simpson was living in the nearby village of Gilmerton. On the 12th of February 1828, the men spotted Simpson in the Grassmarket area of the city, which was near to their home. It was clear to the men that Abigail Simpson had been drinking that day. The men approached the woman and convinced her to come back to the lodging house for a few more drinks. Already being in a drunken state, Simpson agreed and followed the men back to the house at Tanner's Close.

As the three people began to get to know one another over a dram of whisky, Abigail Simpson, told the men that she had a daughter and Burke told her that he was single and was looking for love. She found the men charming and caring. She then told them that she had come into the city to collect her pension, but some of that money had already been spent on drink. Burke and Hare must have thought that they were quid's in, as they could steal her pension and make even more money by selling her body to the anatomist.

William Burke and William Hare, patiently waited until Abigail Simpson had passed out before they killed her in the same manner as Joseph. They placed her frail body in a tea chest and moved it to Surgeon's Square where they received another £10 from Dr Knox.

PEDLAR – "A travelling salesman who walked from town to village, selling their items".

Collinsdictionary.com

The next victim of Burke and Hare was a male English traveller or pedlar as it was known back then and that in February 1928. The travelling salesman who was lodging with the Hares was suffering from jaundice and Hare did not want to make his lodging house look bad, with all the sick people inside, so they decided to finish him off. Again, they went out and brought a tea chest to place his body inside and then sold his remains to Dr Knox.

Instead of looking for people who were close to dying, they decided to change their ways and approach people that would not be missed by anyone.

JAUNDICE – "It's a disease that turns your skin and the whites of your eyes yellow. New-born babies often get it. But adults can, too".

Webmd.com

Whilst walking around Edinburgh on the 9th of April 1828, William Burke stumbled across two women named Mary Paterson and Janet Brown.

Mary Paterson was born on the 7th of February 1808 to parents William Paterson and Margaret King. She was baptised on the 15th of February 1808 at Saint Cuthbert's church in Edinburgh. This information can be seen in Scotland, Select Births and Baptisms, 1564-1950.

William Burke began talking to the women and asked if they would like some breakfast. Instead of taking the women back to Hare's lodging house, Burke decided to take them to his brother Constantine's house in Gibb's Close. Arriving at his brother's house, the trio was greeted by Constantine and his wife Elizabeth. Constantine was leaving for work, so Elizabeth cooked breakfast for them, by using up most of the food supply for the week, however, she did not seem to mind because of the idea of William Burke socialising with another woman instead of Helen McDougal was great for him. It seems like Elizabeth Burke and Helen McDougal did not get on well with each other.

During the hours of conversation, William Burke got to know Janet Brown rather well. Mary Paterson passed out due to the whisky rather early on in the day. It is believed that her body could not take much drink. Burke was hoping that Janet Brown would pass out, for a two for one deal with Dr Knox, however, she liked her drink and could drink a lot before feeling the effects.

As lunchtime approached, Burke and Janet Brown left Mary Paterson at the house in Gibbs Close and went out for lunch.

Pretending to woo Janet Brown, Burke told her that he was single and had an important job that paid a good wage. Brown was delighted by this, as Burke had shown her and her friend much kindness throughout the day.

When the couple returned to his brother's lodgings, they were part way through a conversation when Helen McDougal walked in and began screaming at William Burke. She claimed that she was his wife and Janet Brown apologised and left the home, hoping to go back later to pick up her friend. By this point, whisky was thrown around the room and screams from both Burke and McDougal could be heard, however, Mary Paterson, who was still fast asleep in a drunken haze did not stir. William Burke eventually kicked his common-law wife out of the house.

Helen McDougal decided to take drastic measures and went to collect their friends William Hare and his wife Margaret. When they arrived in Gibb's Close, William Hare sent the women out of the house, while he and Burke decided on what to do with Mary Paterson. Killing her in the normal manner, the men took her body to Dr Knox.

Due to the suspicion of their partners, it was time that they had to come clean to their wives and tell them about their new 'hobby'. They received eight pounds for Paterson's body and when her friend Janet Brown came back to look for her, they said that she left and headed south.

Unfortunately, when Dr Knox when he displayed Mary Paterson's body on the table, his students recognised her as either Mary Connelly or Mary Paterson. It was the assumption that Mary Paterson was a local prostitute but that was not the case.

Mary had spent the past three years of her life living in the Magdalene Asylum in Canongate, Edinburgh. She was sent there because while working as a servant, the head of the household got her pregnant. Her family chose not to disclose the pregnancy and the Magdalene Asylum is where a pregnant woman would be sent. The women had to spend at least three years there and would work to pay for their upkeep. As soon as possible Mary wanted to leave and asked for permission to be released, however, up to her release date, she began to experience pain in her stomach. She fell ill rather quickly and was taken to the hospital, where she was seen by these students just a few days before her death.

She was in the hospital with a woman named Mary Connelly, which is why the students could not remember her surname. However, while Mary was treated for a liver issue, Mary Connelly passed away. Meaning that this woman could only be Mary Paterson.

It seems that when she was released into Edinburgh, just a day before her murder, she was still suffering from her illness. This is probably one of the reasons why Mary could not drink much alcohol. On top of that, she was in an asylum for three years and was fully sober.

Dr Knox liked the beauty of Mary; he paid an artist to come into the room and draw a sketch of her looking alive and fully naked. This was not a normal thing that anatomist did in the 1800s.

It seems like Janet Brown did not believe in the tale she was told about Mary Paterson's whereabouts. On the occasion that she would see Constantine Burke on the streets, she would ask him where Mary was, much to his annoyance.

Magdalene Asylum

Magdalene Asylums were built for young women, who found themselves in pregnancy out of wedlock. The women who entered the facilities had to spend three years living in the establishment until they could ask permission to leave.

The first Magdalene Asylum in Edinburgh opened in 1797 in Canongate, which would have been situated next to the Canongate Kirk. At the same time as this opening, an Asylum was opened in Glasgow. These buildings were funded by charitable donations from the local churches and elsewhere, including private donations. Originally the building was set up as a halfway house, for women who had been sentenced to spend time in prison. However, they soon began taking in unexpected pregnant women, girls and women who had no one else to look after them and women who wanted to get out of prostitution.

Where Magdalene Asylum was situated

Canongate was a known area that prostitutes would find their customs. The area was underprivileged and many people lived hand to mouth, meaning as soon as they earned their money, it would soon be gone. In the early 19th century, there were around 200 brothels in the city of Edinburgh. It was around this time that the clientele began to move from the deprived people to the merchants and nobles.

Of course, you did not live at the Magdalene Asylum for free, the women and girls who lived there had to work for their keep, mostly doing the laundry, sewing and cleaning the building.

Due to the number of women entering the Asylums, the establishment on Canongate was closed in 1842 and was moved to Leafy Dalry on the other side of town, where it would house more women. The building on Canongate was left to fall apart with age and was eventually torn down.

The Magdalene Asylum continued to flourish in Ireland until the 1960s. However, by this time the houses had gained a bad reputation for themselves.

After Helen McDougal and Margaret Laird heard about what their husbands were up to, Margaret decided to help them along the way. While working in the stables on the day, fixing shoes, Margaret Laird, brought an unknown woman back to the lodging house, under the impression that they would spend the day drinking. The woman drank continuously and Margaret placed her into bed several times, however, she refused to sleep. On returning home William Hare saw his next victim and killed her by himself. By the time that William Burke came into the house, he was shocked to see what had occurred that day and stated that he did not recognise the lady. This would be William Hare's 'first' killing without his friend.

In May 1828, an old beggar lady named Effie or sometimes spelt Effy was their next victim. Effie was someone who was known to William Burke, she had sold him scraps of leather previously, while he worked as a cobbler. Burke brought Effie back to the stables. He probably told her that he wanted to buy some leather. While there he gave her a drink of whisky. They were soon joined by William Hare. Placing a cloth over Effie's face, they killed the poor woman and sold her body to Dr Knox. They received ten pounds for her body.

After the murder of Effie, William Burke was near a shop at West Port when he spotted a local Police Officer named Andrew Williamson, who was escorting a drunken woman back to her home to sober up. Burke saw this as an opportunity. He did not even have to get this woman drunk.

William Burke walked over to the Policeman and started a conversation. In it, he told the Officer that it was a waste of his time to be taking drunk people home and that he knew the woman and would do it himself. Pleasantly surprised the Officer agreed and walked off, leaving Burke with his next victim. Instead of taking his stranger home, he decided to take her back to the lodging house for more drink. There he ended her life, put her body in a tea chest and sold it to Dr Knox.

TEA CHEST - A tea chest is a large wooden box in which tea is packed when it is exported. People also use tea chests for putting things in when they move from one house to another.
Collinsdictionary.com

In June of 1828, a blind Grandmother and death and dumb Grandson arrived in Edinburgh from Glasgow. The woman to the city to visit a friend. While walking around Edinburgh, William Burke spotted the two and thought that they would be easy targets. As the woman and Burke began talking, she mentioned her friend and the address and Burke stated that this person was staying at his house and that he would take her there. As William Burke led the two back to Tanner's Close, they arrived and the 'friend' was not there (of course not because Burke lied), so he poured the woman, a glass of whisky, while they waited.

Before long the grandmother began to feel tired. Burke took her into one of the rooms to lie down and rest. Around this time, William Hare arrived back home to see that Burke had not one but two people present. Burke and Hare crept back into the bedroom and finished the lady off, then they stripped her clothes.

The woman's Grandson was not used to not being by his grandmother's side and slowly began to get agitated. The men thought about what they were going to do with the boy and decided that it was best for them to kill him also. The men took the boy into the same room as his deceased Grandmother and killed him. However, how they killed him has two different stories. William Burke claimed in one of his confessions that he killed the lady in the normal manner, however, word began to circulate that they lent the boy over and broke his back. I believe in the 'burking' manner was the cause of this boy's death. It seems unrealistic to change the way of murdering when it seems flawless.

After the deed, the men decided that two bodies would not fit into a tea chest and decided to go out and buy a barrel. On returning home, they managed to get both of the bodies inside and placed the barrel overnight in the stables. The next day they realised that the barrel would be too heavy to carry to Surgeon' Square, so they decided to use Hare's horse and cart, to transport the 'goods' across town.

It was now night time and fewer people were on the street. They placed the barrel onto the cart and began their journey. It was not long before the horse had refused to move anymore. By now, William Hare began to get angry with his animal and hit it several times. Still, the horse would move no more. By now the people on the street were beginning to watch the men and stare. This made them nervous, so Hare got down and pulled the horse to Surgeon's Square. The men collected £16 for the two bodies.

Back at the lodging house, William Hare took his disgraced horse back to the stables where he shot it for refusing to move. Was this Hare showing his true colours or was he that frustrated?

William Burke would later claim that the murders of the young boy and his elderly Grandmother haunted him the most. By now guilt had built up and he began to suffer from insomnia. To help get him some rest, he spent days drinking even heavier and increased his dosage of Laudanum.

Laudanum

Laudanum is a type of painkiller that contains Opium, which is also classed as morphine.

This drug was cheaper to buy than whisky and was easy to get hold of. It was found by a Swiss-German in the 16th century in hopes of helping with severe pain. However, Laudanum is an easily addictive medication, which was not known at the time and the people who found themselves taking it had to eventually increase their dosage to feel the relief. One famous man who was addicted to Laudanum was U.S President Abraham Lincoln's wife Mary Todd Lincoln. Researchers into Todd Lincoln's life claimed that the medication gave her visions of Indian men coming to kill her.

By the 20th century, it had become known the side effects and how deadly the drug was. By now you could not buy it anywhere and had to see a doctor for a prescription. However, Opium is still around and in use.

Mrs Elizabeth Haldane was Burke and Hare's next victim. Elizabeth had at least two daughters Mary Ann and Margaret, who was named Peggy for short. She raised the family in Glasgow, as a single parent, however, for unknown circumstances the three Haldane women found themselves moving to the city of Edinburgh.

Elizabeth had been lodging with the Hares since the spring of 1828. One day during the early summer months, she had come back to the lodging-house, intoxicated with alcohol. Not being able to manage to get to the house, she found herself in the stable, where she passed out on some straw. Unfortunately, she was found by William Burke and William Hare in this state and she was killed in the same manner. This is now the killer's modus operandi (the way that they killed their victims). However, within a matter of weeks Elizabeth Haldane's daughter Margaret 'Peggy' went to the lodging house to look for her mother.

Burke and Hare convinced 'Peggy' to come inside and wait for her mother, as they expressed that she would be back any minute. Beginning to panic, they decided to get the whisky out and keep offering it to the young woman until she too became too intoxicated to fight back. 'Peggy' was soon killed. Both of the Haldane's remains were taken to 10 Surgeons Square and sold to now the infamous Dr Knox.

Around June, William Hare mentioned to Burke that he thought that they should murder Helen McDougal. William Burke must have had strong feelings for McDougal, as he kept on trying to avoid Hare's comments. In this month, a relative of McDougal, a woman named Ann McDougal showed up in Edinburgh and decided to stay with the couple. To try and get Hare off his back about killing his partner, Burke offered up Ann instead of Helen. After getting Ann McDougal drunk, the men approached her in her slumber and killed her.

In late June of 1828, William Burke decided to take his common-law wife Helen 'Nelly' went to Falkirk to visit her family. In his confessions, Burke made a statement that they used to do this trip at the same time every year to watch a parade. It is possible that this parade was something to do with the Battle of Bannockburn.

Did William Burke do this to protect Helen McDougal or did he feel a change within himself? Was he losing control? Maybe he planned to stay in Falkirk with Helen and leave the memory of Edinburgh behind. However, after a few weeks away, Burke and McDougal travelled back into the city and when they arrived at the Log's Lodging House, he found his friend, Hare, acting strangely.

Before Burke left for his trip, he and Hare agreed not to kill or sell the bodies alone. It may be plausible that they made this pact because if one got caught, the other would have to go down too. William Burke asked Hare what he had been doing while he was away. Looking suspicious, Burke then asked him if he had sold any bodies to the Doctor. Hare told Burke that he had not sold any bodies to Dr Knox and he had his word. However, Burke did not believe this and eventually made an excuse to leave the house alone.

William Burke slowly walked to 10 Surgeons Square, where he knocked on the door and asked to speak to Dr Knox. Was it in the back of Burke's mind that his close friend would never betray him and was he thinking that his mind was beginning to play tricks on him, as he had seen so much killing in the past months? Dr Knox approached Buke inside the building and stated that he had paid William Hare a sum of eight pounds for a women's body. This revelation shocked Burke and he got angry. He rushed back to the lodging-house, where he confronted Hare and told him that he and Helen McDougal will be moving out that day. Wanting to make amends Hare attempted to apologise and even offered William Burke some money, but it was no use. Burke and his wife, packed up their little belongings and went to the Guest House of John Brogan. This suited William Burke, as he was forced to pay Margaret Laird £1 per person that he murdered in her home.

John Brogan

John Brogan lived between Grindlays Close and Weavers Close, which is on the same side of the road as Tanner's Close. Looking at the map, it was on the same side of the street, just a row down from the Hare's lodging house in West Port. It is unknown where the actual address was for John Brogan's lodging house, but we know the proximity of it.

Nothing much is known about John Brogan. However, we do know that he had an unusual face due to a childhood incident, where he was badly burnt. To help cover up his scars, his parents took him to see a doctor and the only thing the Doctor could do at the time was to pull his lower lip down towards his neck, covering his chin. This procedure gave John a reverse brace and his teeth grew out at a 90-degree angle. As you can imagine, once you had seen John Brogan, you would never forget who he is.

John Brogan rented his home. It seems that his father lived in the same location in the years before. He lived with his wife and it is unknown if he had any children.

Brogan outlived William Burke by five years, passing away from cholera in 1834 in Edinburgh. Because his face was so unusual, a death mask was made from his face and his skull was donated to The Royal College of Surgeons without his family's permission. Within the next few years, his brother came across his brother's skull and told the college that he wanted it buried with his body. The College kindly gave the skull back to the family; however, it was not buried as his brother suggested. He decided to sell the item to a dentist, who then donated it back to the College in 1869. Since then, the skull has been placed on display in the Surgeons' Hall Museum in Edinburgh.

Researchers claimed that John Brogan's wife was a relative of William Burke from Ireland. Although nothing is known about her.

L.A Mackay

While William Burke and Helen McDougal were lodging with John Brogan and his wife, he paid £3 for their rent. During the first few weeks of their arrival, John Brogan decided to go away with his family and it seems that William Burke took over the lease.

The quarrel between Burke and Hare did not last long and they made up. The men chose not to live together, as Burke and McDougal were settled in their own lodging house and were earning a bit of extra money.

Before John Brogan left, he had a washer woman named Mrs Ostler or Hostler working for the family. She would become their next victim.

Mrs Ostler was a recent widow after her husband passed away. This is the reason that she began working for the Brogan family in their lodging house. Between June and October 1828, Mrs Ostler was busy working away in the house, washing the clothes. After she had finished work, William Burke convinced Mrs Ostler to have a drink of whisky with him. Giving in to him, she had a cup, then another was poured and another until she was quite merry. She began to sing out loud and dance. By now she began to feel tired, so Burke suggested that she should have a laydown. It was around this time that William Hare, turned up at the Brogan Lodging House and together they crept up to the unsuspecting woman and smothered her. After her murder, Burke and Hare received £8 for her remains from Dr Knox.

The next victim of Burke and Hare was a mentally disabled man named James Wilson. James was nicknamed 'daft Jamie' and was known to the people of Edinburgh. James was homeless, who took to begging on the streets of Edinburgh. Although he had a mother who lived in Stevenlaws Close, Edinburgh, James decided not to live with her because of her aggression. He chose to sleep in doorways during the night. He saw his mother regularly.

Stevenlaws Close

It is claimed that James Wilson was born on the 27th of November 1809 in Edinburgh, however, I cannot find any record for this date. There is a few James Wilsons who was born in 1808, 1810 and 1811. To pinpoint the exact James would be a pure guess.

James Wilson was once described as a harmless young man, who liked his snuff. He chose not to drink alcohol. Even in winter Wilson who was approximately 18 years old at the time, would walk around Edinburgh with no hat and holes in his worn-out shoes.

WHAT IS SNUFF? – "Snuff is tobacco, which is dried and finely ground down. There are two main types of snuff — dried and moist. To use dried snuff, you inhale the ground tobacco into your nasal cavity. To use moist snuff, you put the tobacco between your lower lip or cheek and gum. The nicotine from the tobacco is absorbed through the lining of your nose or mouth".

Healthline.com

L.A Mackay

In November 1828, Margaret Laird or Helen McDougal found the eighteen-year-old James Wilson walking around the streets of West Port, looking for his mother who was a hawker. James' mother would be walking the streets from morning until night, trying to sell her things.

HAWKER – "A Hawker is like a Pedler. They walk around selling small items, sometimes door to door but usually on the streets".
Collinsdictionary.com

The woman approached James and was able to convince him to go back to their lodging where she would send someone to get his mother. Although hesitant James agreed and followed, he back to Log's Lodging House, which was only a short walk away.

Once he arrived at the house, he was greeted by William Burke and William Hare and was given Whisky to drink. However, the men got impatient with James Wilson and his refusal to carry on drinking. This led Burke and Hare to attempt to suffocate him before he was intoxicated. However, the men were caught off guard, as James Wilson fought back. Wilson was a strong and tall teenager. The men eventually managed to overpower James and he was killed, then taken to Dr Knox's house.

When Doctor Knox placed Jamie's body on the dissecting table, his students recognised him from his bad feet and his face. Shocked, rumours began spreading when James was missing from his usual hangouts. To attempt to conceal the identity of his next dissection experiment, Dr Knox, chopped off James feet and his head, in hopes that no one else would recognise the man. It seems that by now Burke and Hare were beginning to get sloppy with their 'work' and instead of killing people who were passing through the city, they began to lure anyone back to their houses, in hopes of a profit.

It was supposedly between this death and the final victim that William Hare killed an unknown woman alone. There is no other information on this death, as what we do know was from the confessions that William Burke had written during his time in jail.

The last victim of killers Burke and Hare was killed on Halloween night on the 31st of October 1828. This time it was a lady named Margaret Docherty. Docherty was a middle-aged woman who came from Northern Ireland.

William Burke began talking to Margaret Docherty at a local shop named Rymer's, where he was having a drink and heard the woman speaking to the worker. He struck up a conversation with this stranger and claimed that his mother's maiden name was Docherty. I cannot find any information to back up with Burke's mother's maiden name was Docherty.

Burke lured the woman to John Brogan's lodging house, stating that a family member should not be alone and that he would care for her and make her some breakfast. As they began to get to know one another, the whisky was placed on the table and they began drinking. As Margaret Docherty began eating, Burke left her with Helen McDougal and went off to find his partner in crime William Hare. He would return a short while later with Hare and Margaret Laird.

As they were all chatting, a suggestion suddenly came up that they should celebrate that night with a party for his long lost relative.

At this time, William Burke had two other lodgers staying in the same room as him named Mr James and Mrs Grey. Not wanted to be disturbed, Burke bribed the Grey lodgers to stay out for the evening, in return for payment. He then took the Grey family to Log's Lodging House, where he paid for a bed for the night. When asked why he wanted them out of the house, Burke stated that a family member had turned up from Ireland and he wanted to spend some time with her alone, to catch up. The Grey's thought that this was unusual, but agreed to spend the night with the Hares.

By nightfall, the party at Broggan's Lodging House was already in full swing. There was food, music, singing, dancing and plenty of alcohol to go around. While dancing Margaret Docherty hurt her foot, this more than likely sobered her up slightly. By between 10 pm and 11 pm, the close neighbours heard some commotion and when they looked into the house, they saw Helen McDougal holding a whisky bottle to Margaret Docherty's mouth. It looked as though; she was trying to ply the woman with as much drink as possible. A short while later an agreement between Burke and Hare began. This was due to the drink that they had consumed and was not out of the ordinary. As the argument carried on, Margaret Docherty stood up and went over to defend William Burke, as he had treated her so kindly that day.it is unknown if it was an accident or something more sinister, but William Hare managed to push Margaret Docherty down to the ground and it seemed that she had injured herself even more. Unable to stand back up either due to her injuries or because of the alcohol Burke and Hare stopped fighting and went over to the woman. It was at this point that Margaret Laird and Helen McDougal ran out of the house and stood in the close waiting for the go-ahead to go back inside.

While in the building William Burke and William Hare killed Margaret Docherty as she laid helpless on the floor. After the men were sure that Docherty was deceased, they took her body over to the bed and undressed her to prepare her for Dr Knox.

Just after midnight John Broggan's son came to the residence and began drinking with them. Fortunately, the body of Docherty must have been concealed by this point, as he did not see anything in relevance to a murder. As the hours passed, the men began to feel tired and soon fell asleep near Margaret Docherty's body.

THE DISCOVERY

The next morning at 9 am, on the 1st of November 1898, William Burke walked a short distance to Log's Lodging House to check on the Grey's. While there he invited them back to the house for breakfast as a thank you for staying somewhere else the night before. When they arrived back at Broggan's Lodging House, they found Helen McDougal and John Broggan talking to two neighbours, who were Mrs Connoway and Mrs Law. The foursome was in the house talking about the event and the night before and the plans for the day.

Mrs Grey asked Helen McDougal where the lady was from the night before. McDougal stated that she had got too intoxicated and they ended up throwing her out of the house during the night. This did not make sense to Mrs Grey, as William Burke went to all the trouble to spend time with the woman, however, she struggled it off.

The Grey's had a child in their care and after eating their breakfast, Mrs Grey walked over to her bed to dress the baby. As she did William Burke began to act strangely. He unexpectedly began to throw whisky around the room, while the Grey's looked oddly at him. It seemed to Mrs Grey that Burke did not want her to go near the bed.

The Grey's began to get suspicious of William Burke and they decided to wait until everyone was out of the house to investigate. During the evening, the lodgers found out that no one was at home. They entered the room and slowly walked over to the bed. As they looked beneath it, the Grey's found Margaret Docherty's deceased and naked body, stuffed into some straw, near the wall.

As you can imagine, this shocked the couple and they decided to go to the police station to let them know what they had found. On the way out of West Port, the couple bumped into Helen McDougal and Margaret Laird. The woman could see that Mr and Mrs Grey looked pale with worry and asked what was wrong. The Grey's told the women what they had found and the reaction with they received would surprise them more. Instead of the women being disgusted with the event, they attempted to bribe the Grey's and offered them £10 a week to not say anything about what they saw in the house. However, this couple knew right from wrong and declined their offer. They probably thought if they could do that to a 'relative' that they would have no problem in killing them. The Grey's then set off to alert the Police.

Helen McDougal and Margaret Laird quickly returned to the home and found William Burke and William Hare there. They told the men about the conversation with the Grey's and Burke and Hare decided to get rid of the body as fast as possible. Buying another tea chest, they returned and squeezed Docherty's body inside and took it to 10 Surgeon's Square. When they arrived at Dr Knox's house, his assistant took the remains and gave them £3, promising them another £5 when Dr Knox returned later on. Being in a hurry, the men had no time to argue and accepted the transaction. They then returned to their houses.

As the Grey's confessed to the Police Officers and told them the story of how the women had tried to bribe them, the Officers, knowing William Burke rather well, thought that they should go along to Broggan's Lodging House to see if there was any evidence, to back up the Grey's story.

As the day was ending, the Police decided to investigate the following day. It is not known how Burke, Hare and their partners spent their final night of freedom.

The following morning, the Policemen arrived at Broggan's Lodging House and asked if they could take a look around. William Burke being friendly with the Police, as his brother worked at the station, kindly agreed. The Policemen made Burke aware of what the Grey's had told them, however, William Burke's story was completely different. He told the Officers that the Grey's had not been keeping up to date with the money for their lodgings, so like any other business owner would do, they kicked them out onto the streets. This comment made sense to the police as retaliation, but they continued to ask Burke questions. William Burke told the Officers that Margaret Docherty left the house at 7 pm the night of the party (31st October).

After a quick search was complete, only one tiny spot of blood was found beneath the bed. Helen McDougal told the Policemen that she had not been able to change it yet, due to a lodger staying there. They could find no more evidence apart from an item of clothing that belonged to McDougal.

The Officers were about to leave when they quickly thought of questioning Helen McDougal about the situation. Upon questioning William Burke and his wife Helen gave two different accounts of when Margaret Docherty left the premises. McDougal claimed that it was 7 am that Margaret Docherty left. This made the Police raise an eyebrow and they left knowing that there was something suspicious going on.

That day one of the Officers knocked on the door of 10 Surgeon Square. Like normal Dr Knox's assistant answered. He Policeman looked at the assistant and asked them if any bodies were delivered for Dr Knox the day earlier. The assistant told them that a woman had been delivered by two men and had arrived in a tea chest. Upon inspecting the remains of the old woman, which was laid in vinegar in hopes of preservation, James Grey was sent for to identify the corpse. He told the Officers that this was the woman Margaret Docherty that they saw alive on the 31st of October and deceased on the 1st of November. It seems like the Police had all the evidence that they had needed to arrest Burke and Hare.

L.A Mackay

Arrest

On the 3rd of November 1828, an arrest warrant was issued to arrest William Burke and Helen McDougal. The Officers went to Broggan's Lodging House and arrested the couple along with John Broggan, who was eventually released for custody. As the day carried on William Hare and Margaret Laird was also taken to the Police Station, along with their baby.

All five suspects were kept apart and asked for statements and were questioned about the death of Margaret Docherty. It turned out that they all had separate stories to tell.

While they were being questioned, two forensic specialists were called to take a look at the body and to give a cause of death. The forensic team was William Newbigging and Robert Christison. Both were professionals and were helped by the Police Surgeon Dr Alexander Black.

Upon investigating the corpse of Margaret Docherty, the men could not see any signs of violence or struggle. There were no marks on the body and eventually classed it as possible suffocation, however, this could not be proven.

Another search was carried out at Broggan's Lodging House and then one at Log's Lodging House, where the Hare's lived. There they found some items of clothing that did not match, what the couples were wearing.

Students from Surgeons Hall began to come forward with stories of how they thought that more bodies were killed and sold to the Doctor. Two of them, in particular, was a woman named Mary Paterson and 'Daft Jamie'. On closer inspection of the clothes that were found in Log's Lodging House, the items were found to have belonged to both of these victims. However, some of James Wilson's clothes were given to Burke's nephews.

By now the murders had become public knowledge in Edinburgh. Many locals entered the two lodging houses and ransacked them, leaving nothing untouched. Were people feeling guilty for not seeing what was going on under their noses? If the students of Dr Knox went to the police earlier, would it have stopped some people from being murdered? Everyone had so many questions, however, there was little evidence to back up the murder clause. It became clear to the Officers that they needed at least one of them on their side, but which one?

Turning King's Evidence

At the time of the murders, William Burke was in his late 30's and was very sick. He was already drugging himself before the murders started in Edinburgh. This was to take away some of his pain. William Hare on the other side was only 21 years old and had a lot of life left him. From their conversations at the station, it was clear to the Officers that William Hare was more open to speaking more and they turned to him for help.

What Is It?

Turning King's Evidence means to plead your guilt for a crime, but to also turn against your accomplices. By giving evidence in court against your accomplices, you will receive the things you would have been offered. This could have been immunity, better life in prison or spared from the death penalty.

In today's term (2021), Queen Elizabeth II is in charge of the United Kingdom, so instead of turning King's evidence, it would be named turning Queen's evidence.

From the case of Burke and Hare, William Hare was offered immunity for his crimes, if he gave evidence against William Burke and Helen McDougal. This meant that Margaret Laird was also immune from the case because William Hare would not be able to give evidence against his wife.

As you can imagine, William Hare jumped at the chance of turning King's evidence against his friends. He could not read or write, so he told an officer his confession and wrote it down for him. According to his confession, Hare blamed the murder of Margaret Docherty solely on William Burke and admitted that he was in the room at the time but did nothing to take the woman's life away from her.

This is the only thing that we know about Hare's confession. Unfortunately, it has been lost to history and it is known that only one person saw both of the confessions of Burke and Hare and decided in his personal opinion that William Hare's confession was the true account. That is why there is a mix up in order of killings.

Even though William Hare and Margaret Laird were immune from the case, they were sent to Carlton Jail for their protection until after William Burke's trial.

Carlton Gaol

Situated under Carlton Hill was the main prison in Edinburgh during the time of Burke and Hare. Carlton Jail opened its doors to the first convicts in 1817. Its main goal was to replace the old tollbooth in the city, which had to be closed down due to its ageing and not enough cells to hold the inmates.

It is thought that the jail was designed by Archibald Elliott around 1814. Elliott was a Scottish architect, who had work on several infamous buildings including churches, jails and castles, making Carlton Jail his fifth main project.

What remains of Carlton Gaol

At the time of the build, Carlton Jail was the largest prison in the whole of Scotland, holding hundreds of convicts in inhumane conditions. It is claimed that the prisoners did not get any exercise, they were left to starve, only having bread and water. On top of this researchers claimed that the inmates were chained to a wall in their cell and were unable to move around. All they had to do is wait and more than likely the next time they would be able to move would be on the day of their death.

Carlton Jail housed the worst offenders in Scotland. In the time of Burke and Hare, most of the prisoners were there while awaiting a death sentence. There had been many people men and women who were convicted to death in jail and the building hosted its very own noose and death room in the later period of its existence. One notable convict was a woman named Jesse King who was a baby farmer.

Baby Farming – *"The practice of baby farming grew up in late Victorian era when there was no effective contraception and great social stigma attached to having a child out of wedlock. Proper adoption agencies and social services didn't exist at this time. Instead, a number of untrained women offered legal fostering and adoption services to unmarried mothers who would hand over their baby plus, say 10 to 15 pounds in cash (quite a large sum of money then) to them in the hope that the child would be re-homed".*

Capitalpunishmentuk.org

Jesse King would take young children into her care, who were either unwanted or the mother could not provide for the child. King and her husband quickly began to run out of room in their house and came up with the idea of killing off some of the children, so that they could take in more. However, the couple were sloppy about it and one child was found dead in an alleyway. She was finally arrested in 1889 and was sentenced to death at Carlton Jail, which was carried out on the 11th of March 1889 at 8 am by James Berry. Although her husband denied any knowledge of what was going on in the house, recent authors claimed that Jesse King could have been covering for her husband in fear of retaliation. We do not know how many children were murdered by King but she has gone down in history as the last woman to be executed in Edinburgh.

The jail itself was opened 115 years before it became clear that no refurbishment could impact the building to make a difference. The HM Edinburgh Prison was built to replace the run-down Carlton Jail, which opened its door in 1920. From this time, Carlton Jail was left to ruin, along with the graveyard which was once within the grounds and contained the bodies of the executed criminals.

Only a small portion of the Jail can be seen today. It is now named The Governors

House or St Andrew's House and is part of the Scottish Government. The torrents are the sole surviving part of the infamous building and the graveyard that once stood there, which contained the numbers of the prisoners, is now a car park.

THE TRIAL OF 1829

With William Hare and Margaret Laird being immune from prosecution the case of William Burke and Helen MacDougal took place on the 24th of December 1828 in the Parliament House in Edinburgh.

The couple was charged with three murders during their spree; Mary Paterson, James Wilson and Margaret Docherty. At this point, it was unknown to the authorities if William Burke had killed and sold anymore remains or how long it had been going on.

As the proceedings began to take place, the street of Edinburgh was crowded by onlookers, who wanted to know every detail about the case. The ordinary people had already convinced themselves that William Burke and Helen MacDougal were guilty and waited to see what sort of punishment they would get.

The men who would be hearing the case was;

- Lord Justice Clerk – Lord David Boyle
- Lord Gullies – Adam Gullies
- Lord Alloway – David Cathcart
- Lord Meadowbank – Alexander Maconochie
- Lord Pitmilly - David Monypenny
- Lord Mackenzie – Joshua Henry Mackenzie

- William Burke's representative - 9th Baronet Sir James Wellwood Moncreiff

Originally 55 people were called to the courtroom to be questioned about the couple, however, from the beginning Helen MacDougal's defence team, which consisted of Henry Cockburn, Mark Napier, Hugh Bruce, George Patton. James Beveridge, W. S. one of the Agents for the Poor Agent, spoke to the court and told them that Helen MacDougal only appears in one of the three cases against her.

"...If it shall be decided that the prisoner is obliged to answer to this indictment at all, her answer to it is, that she is not 6 guilty, aud that the Prosecutor cannot prove the facts on which his charge rests. But she humbly submits that she is not bound to plead to it. She is accused of one murder committed in October 1828, in a house in Portsburgh, and of no other offence. Yet she is placed in an indictment along with a different person, who is accused of other two murders, each. of them committed at a different time, and at a different place, — it not being alleged that she had any connexion with either of these crimes. This accumulation of pannels and of of- fences is not necessary for public justice, and exposes the accused to intolerable prejudice, and is not warranted, so far as 1 can be ascertained, even by a single precedent."

The defence team of MacDougal (1828)

Taking this into consideration, the Lord Justice Clerk, decided that the prosecution should pick just one murder to go forward for this case, leading for the Judge to single out the trials.

After careful consideration, the prosecution declared that the case they would like to prosecute William Burke and Helen MacDougal over was the killing of Margaret Docherty. This was the only case that involved MacDougal and it was their only source of actual evidence since the body of Margaret Docherty was found at 10 Surgeon's Square. This brought the number of witnesses down significantly to eighteen. These people were;

1. **James Braidwood** – The man who created the map of the streets and William Burke's room
2. **Mary Stewart** – Owned a lodging house which Michael (Margaret Docherty's son) stayed
3. **Charles M'Lauchlan** – Lodging in Mary Stewart's house
4. **William Noble** – Worked at Rymers shop
5. **Ann (Black) Conway** – Neighbour of William Burke and Helen MacDougal
6. **Janet (Lawrie) Law** - Neighbour of William Burke and Helen MacDougal
7. **Hugh Alston** - Neighbour of William Burke and Helen MacDougal
8. **Elizabeth Paterson** – Brother David worked for Dr Knox
9. **David Paterson** - Worked for Dr Knox
10. **John Brogan** – Friend or relative of Helen MacDougal
11. **Mrs Grey** – Lodged with William Burke and Helen MacDougal
12. **James Grey** - Lodged with William Burke and Helen MacDougal
13. **John M'Culloch** - Worked as a porter for Burke
14. **John Fisher** – Worked for Edinburgh Police
15. **William Hare** – Committed the crimes with Burke
16. **Margaret (Hare) Laird** – Wife of William Hare
17. **Mr Black** - Worked as a local Doctor in Edinburgh
18. **Dr Christison** – Worked as a Pathologist

When asked separately if they were guilty of the crime or not, William Burke and Helen MacDougal declared that they were both not guilty. After that fifteen of the town's men were sworn in to be the jury for the trial, their names were;

1. **Nicol Allan,** who was the Manager of Hercules Insurance Company in Edinburgh.
2. **John Paton** worked as a builder.
3. **James Trench** worked as a builder.
4. **Peter M'Gregor,** worked as a merchant.
5. **William Bonar,** who worked as a banker.
6. **James Banks,** who worked as an agent, Cassillis Place, Leith Walk,
7. **James Melliss** worked as a merchant in Edinburgh.
8. **John MTie,** who worked as a merchant in Leith.
9. **Thomas Barker** worked as a brewer.
10. **Henry Fenwick** was a grocer in Dunbar.
11. **David Brash** worked as a grocer in Leith.
12. **David Hunter,** whose occupation was an ironmonger in Edinburgh.

13. **Robert Jeffrey**, who was an engraver.
14. **William Bell** worked as a grocer in Dunbar.
15. **William Robertson**, whose occupation was a cooper in Edinburgh.

The Witnesses

The trial documents themselves is just short of two hundred pages, filled with repeated questions and responses. For this book, we have decided to reduce the size of the document and to write the highlights of what happened.

James Braidwood

The first person to be called a witness was a man named James Braidwood. Braidwood was sworn in by the Lord Justice Clerk. He was only on the stand for a matter of minutes because he was the man who drew and described the room which William Burke and Helen MacDougal lived in and he also drew the streets, showing where the location of the house was. The court as Braidwood to confirm that these drawings that they showed him, were drawn by his hand. He agreed they were and was then asked to leave.

Mary Stewart

Mary Stewart was sworn in by Lord Pitmilly. Stewart had owned her own lodging house and she spent most of her time in court speaking about Margaret Docherty's son Michael, who had lodged with her for approximately two months before the arrival of his mother. Michael left the establishment on the 30th of October 1828. At the time that this was happening, Mary Stewart was in hospital being treated for an

L.A Mackay

illness.

She was told that an elderly woman came to the lodging house, looking for Michael. The woman gave her name as Madgy Campbell and she lodged at the house that night and left the following morning (31st October) to look around the city for her son.

Mary Stewart described what the woman was wearing that day and spoke to the court about identifying her body on Sunday 2nd November.

Where Burke and MacDougal's trial took place

Charles M'Lauchlan

Charles M'Lauchlan confirmed that he was staying in the lodging house of Mary Stewart at the time of Michael's stay. He notifies the court that he had spent some time with the elderly woman, who called herself Majory M'Gonegal. However, M'Lauchlan claimed that the woman had stated that she went by the name of Campbell and Duffie too. Duffie was the surname of her second husband. He stated that the woman was an Irishwoman from Donnegal.

M'Lauchlan worked at a shop of St Mary's Wynd. He explained that the woman had come to see him in his shop on Saturday and told M'Lauchlan that she would be leaving town, as she could not find her son.

William Noble

William Noble was the fourth person to give evidence in the case of William Burke and Helen MacDougal.

Noble worked as a 'shop boy' at Rymer's shop in West Port. The address for the shop was given as 10 Portsburgh. He told the court that he knew both William Burke and William Hare and that they frequently entered the shop.

When the Irish woman came into the shop on Friday 31st October to ask for some charity, Burke asked the lady her name and stated that she must have been a relation of his mother. William Burke offered the woman breakfast at his house and she followed him out of the shop.

Noble last saw William Burke the next day, when he entered the shop between five and six in the evening, to buy a tea box. Mrs Hare (Margaret Laird) then came to pick the box up.

Ann (Black) Conway

Ann Conway was sworn into court by Lord Meadowbank. Conway was a neighbour of William Burke and Helen MacDougal. It is mentioned that she lived in the first door on the right that you came to as you walked into the passage. She had just one room.

Ann Conway told the court that she saw Burke with a woman on Friday 31st October in the morning. They walked past her house, as they headed towards Burke's. She went around to Burke's house and found the elderly lady sitting by the fire, eating porridge. As Ann Conway was speaking to Helen MacDougal, she asked who the woman was and MacDougal claimed that she was a relative of Burkes.

After finishing her breakfast, Margaret Docherty told the people in the house, that she needed to see a friend at St Mary's Wynd. Conway advised the woman not to go because she did not know if she would be able to find her way back to the passage and did not want her to get lost.

For a short time, Burke and Docherty spoke about their memories of Ireland before she left, telling them that she would be back later on in the day.

Later that day William Burke, Helen MacDougal and the unknown woman went to see Ann Conway at her home. They were joined by Ann Conway's husband John and William Hare and his wife Margaret Laird. Everyone in the house was drinking and rather merry. There was lots of dancing and singing. Margaret Docherty hurt her foot during the process but carried on regardless.

After an hour or so, Burke, Hare and their partners left and they all went round to William Burke's house. Soon after they left Conway's home, Ann Conway and her husband John went to bed between ten and eleven pm. After being in bed for a short while, the couple was disturbed by what sounded like fighting. The noise came from Burke's house. Despite what Ann and John Conway heard that night they did not leave their house.

At around three in the morning, Ann Conway woke to prepare the open fire for her husband who would wake an hour later for work. She then began to make his breakfast before returning to bed until 8 am.

Sixty minutes after Ann Conway woke for the day, Helen MacDougal knocked on the door. MacDougal told Ann Conway that William Burke would like to see her, so she went along with Helen MacDougal to their lodging house. When she arrived, she found Burke in the presence of John Brogan and Janet Law. By this time, it was 9.15 am and Burke already had a bottle of spirits in his hand. William Burke poured Ann Conway a glass and she drank it. For some reason, Burke began to throw the drink around the room, much to everyone's surprise.

Ann Conway asked MacDougal where the Irishwoman was. Helen MacDougal claimed that the woman was getting 'over friendly' with Burke, so she had kicked her out of the house.

Later that day, Mrs Grey who was lodging with the Burke's, with her husband and her child, approached Ann Conway and guided her to the lodging house, where she and her husband James had spotted a deceased body of Margaret Docherty, however, she saw nothing but straw.

Ann Conway then told the court that before Mrs Grey went to see her around 8 pm, Helen MacDougal spoke to her and suggested that the Greys had been stealing items from inside her home. She mentioned that they would be going out and asked Conway to watch to see if the Greys go into the lodging house. Ann Conway agreed to keep an eye out for her.

Janet (Lawrie) Law

Janet Law lived in the same passageway as Ann Conway, William Burke and Helen MacDougal.

She told the jury that on the 31st of October, she was at Mrs Conway's house at around one in the afternoon. There she saw William Burke, Helen MacDougal and the elderly woman.

That evening Janet Law saw them all again between six and seven pm. Janet Law claimed it looked like they were all having a good time, drinking and dancing and generally having a good time.

By 9.30 pm that night, Janet Law was back in her own house and was in bed. The next thing that Law was aware of was the sound of fighting or scuffling. When she was asked if she could any voices, she replied that she could and she was then asked if she knew whose voice she could hear, she replied that it was the voice of William Burke.

The next morning Helen MacDougal went to Janet Law's house and they began to have a conversation. In the few minutes that the women spoke, MacDougal asked Law if she had heard any arguments or fighting from the night before. It is unknown how Janet Law responded to Helen MacDougal, however, the topic of the elderly lady was brought up. Helen MacDougal again claimed that Margaret Docherty was getting too friendly with Burke and she ended up kicking her out of the house. Helen MacDougal then left and returned an hour later at 9 am. During the second conversation, MacDougal asked to borrow a dram glass. Law took a glass around to their lodgings. When she arrived, she saw William Burke, William Hare, Helen MacDougal and John Brogan. It is unknown if Margaret Laird was there at that time. During her visit, the Grey family had returned to Burke's house and around this time, William Burke decided to sprinkle alcohol around the house.

Soon, Mrs Conway arrived and also spotted Burke's strange behaviour. When asked why he was throwing his drink around the house, William Burke claimed because no one would drink with him.

Fast forward to the Sunday, a day later, Janet Law told the court that she identified the body of an elderly lady at the police station and it was the woman who had been in Burke's house on Friday night.

When Law was cross-examined by the Dean of Faculty. It became clear that the pile of straw which was situated at the bottom of the bed, which hid the body of Margaret Docherty was the place where the Grey's slept.

Hugh Alston

Hugh Alston lived in the flat above William Burke and Helen MacDougal, while Burke lived in the 'sunken flat' below the shop.

Alston was sworn into the courtroom by Judge Mackenzie. When questioned he admitted that on the evening of the 31st of October at 11.30 pm, he was interrupted by the sound of fighting off two men. It only became strange to him when he heard the sound of an unknown woman crying out the word 'murder'. Alston and his wife left their flat and ventured down the stone steps outside. There they stopped halfway down to see if they could see anything. Upon seeing nothing in the area Hugh Alston carried on down the steps and into the passage.

On the ground level, he continued to hear the fighting for about one minute. However, he did not hear a physical fight, but then the sound came of something being strangled, however, he could not work out if the noise came from a human or an animal.

The two men were now speaking to one another quite loudly. The female voice which he had heard before cried out 'murder' again and did so half a dozen times. This caused Hugh Alston to try and look for a policeman. After a few minutes, it came apparent that Alston could not find an officer and upon his return to the passage, he heard a short cry and then nothing else except footsteps.

A juror asked the permission of the court to ask the next question. This was agreed by the Lord Justice Clerk. He asked Hugh Alston, how far away he was standing at the time from William Burke's house, Alston claimed he was approximately three yards away. The juror asked how far Burke's door was away from the passage and he replied fifteen feet.

Between seven and eight pm on Saturday evening, Hugh Alston heard the news that a body had been found inside William Burke's house. It was upon hearing this news that Hugh Alston remembered the strange occurrence from the night before.

Elizabeth Paterson

Elizabeth Paterson lived in the Wester Portsburgh (West Port) area. When she entered the stand, she told the court that she had last seen William Burke on Friday 31st of October. At 10 o'clock, Burke went to Paterson's door and asked to see her brother David, who she lived with. Elizabeth told William Burke that David was not in the house and he thanked her and left.

The next day David Paterson asked his sister Elizabeth to go to Burke's house. She agreed but was unsure which house William Burke lived in. As she entered the passage, Elizabeth saw Mrs Law and asked her the directions.

David Paterson

David Paterson was sworn into court by Lord Pitmilly.

David was the brother of the last witness Elizabeth Paterson. He spoke to the court and told them that he lived at 26 West Port and he worked as a keeper at the museum which was run by Dr Knox.

Returning home around 12, David Paterson spotted William Burke banging on his door looking for him. As Paterson began to speak to Burke, Burke suggested that he should make his way to his lodgings. When Paterson arrived at William Burke's house, he spotted William Hare and their partners in the men's company. He walked into the room and William Burke asked David Paterson to pass a message on to Dr Knox, telling him in a low voice that he had something for him, while pointing to the bottom of the bed, where a lump of straw was seen on the floor.

David Paterson told the court, that he understood what William Burke meant, which to him was a deceased body, however, he would not be able to prove it. He agreed to pass on the message, greeting Burke goodnight and left the property.

At 9 am the next morning, William Burke turned up at the Paterson door once again. It was clear that David Paterson did not want to get involved with whatever Burke was doing and told the man that if he had a message for the Doctor, he should go there and tell him himself. William Burke agreed and walked away.

The next time that David Paterson saw William Burke was in Dr Knox's room along with his assistant. This would have been between 12 and 2 that day. At 7 pm that night, William Burke, William Hare and a porter named M'Culloch brought a package to 10 Surgeons Square for Dr Knox. The item was placed in an old tea chest. David Paterson and Dr Knox's assistant was ordered by the Doctor to escort the package down to the cellar, after which the men headed towards Newington, to the home of Dr Knox, where they would be given five pounds. This was not all of the money. The men were told to come back on Monday to pick up the rest of the money which was owed to them.

However, by Sunday at 7 am, Sergeant Major Fisher and Lieutenant Paterson held a conversation with David Paterson. The Officers asked Paterson if the Doctor had received any new deliveries in the past couple of days. David Paterson agreed that he had and all three walked down to Surgeons Square, where they could see for themselves. Upon opening the box that contained Docherty's body, it became clear that this was not a grave robbing, the body of an elderly female had not been yet buried. On inspecting the remains, they found no marks but did see a little bit of blood which seemed to have come out of the mouth.

John Brogan

John Brogan admitted to the court that he was with William Burke on Friday 31st of October from 4 pm until 7 pm, along with the usual people which were William Hare, Helen MacDougal (who he called his aunt) and Margaret Laird. However, this time Burke had a guest, which was an elderly woman.

At 7 pm, John Brogan separated himself from the rest and returned much later on at 2 am. At this point, the old woman was nowhere to be seen. William Hare and Margaret Laird were on the bed, while William Burke and Helen MacDougal were standing next to the window quietly speaking to one another. Eventually, Brogan fell asleep in the room, along with the others for the night.

The next morning, John Brogan woke and left the house at 7 am and returned two hours later at 9 am. By this time the Grey family had arrived. John Brogan admitted to the court, that he heard a woman ask about the elderly woman, who was with them the night before. He heard that the men got into a fight and the elderly woman began shouting 'MURDER', so, Helen MacDougal kicked her out of their home. It was at this time that Burke began spraying alcohol over their room.

Mrs Grey

Mrs Grey was sworn into the court by Lord Meadowbank. She was asked if she knew the prisoners William Burke and Helen MacDougal, Mrs Grey declared that she did and was lodging with them for just under a week.

When speaking about the 31st of October, Mrs Grey explained that she saw a lady there, whose name was Docherty. The woman looked poor and was wearing a dark gown and a red striped nightdress underneath her everyday clothing.

William Burke told Mrs Grey that he had met the woman at 9 am that morning. During the day, the Grey's were told to leave the house for the night between five and six pm. William Burke had arranged to lodge them at William Hare's house with that arranged Margaret (Hare) Laird, walked the family around to their house in Tanner's Close.

That night around 9 pm, Mrs Grey returned to Burke's house to pick up some clothes for their child. She saw a party in full swing, along with singing and dancing. The elderly woman was still in the house at this point. She quickly walked in, picked up the clothing and left.

The next time Mrs Grey saw William Burke was the next morning when he walked around to their lodgings to collect them and he invited them for breakfast. They all returned to Burke's lodgings and when they arrived the room was full. Burke's neighbours Mrs Conway and Mrs Law were present, along with John Brogan, William Hare and Margaret Laird.

Noticing that the elderly woman was not in the room, Mrs Grey asked of her whereabouts. Helen MacDougal claimed that she had kicked her out of the house during the evening.

During her visit, Mrs Grey walked over to the pile of straw that was situated over by the bed, at this point William Burke began to act unusually. He asked her what she was doing and she claimed that she was looking for her child's stockings. He began to make a show of himself and threw drink around the room, even under the bed, where he began to pour the alcohol into a cup.

Mrs Grey and her family came and went from their lodging house two or three times that day, upon their return, they found John Brogan sat in the room on a chair. He told Mrs Grey that he was told to sit there until William burke returned and to not let anyone near the bed.

As the sun was setting in the sky, Mrs Grey and the servant girl who worked for Mrs Law entered the lodging house of William Burke and Helen MacDougal. Mrs Grey took it upon herself to investigate and found the deceased naked body of an elderly lady with her right arm being the first part that she would see. As Mr Grey arrived, he lifted the straw that covered the body and he saw a small amount of blood on the woman's face. The couple were so shocked that they dropped the straw and left the premises. Near the stone steps to the passage, they came face to face with Helen MacDougal.

Mr Grey asked MacDougal about the body that they had found near the bed. She attempted to bribe the couple with a few shillings, which eventually changed to £10 a week. She asked the couple not to say anything. Helen MacDougal seemed to get slightly high rated and told the Grey's to "Hold your tongue", however, the couple ignored her bribery and headed towards the police station.

Mr and Mrs Grey would later identify the body as the elderly woman who was singing in Burke's house that Friday evening.

James Grey

On the stand, James Grey backed up his wife's story and again would repeat what she had said when she took to the stand.

John M'Culloch

John M'Culloch was sworn in by Lord Pitmilly. M'Culloch spoke of his occupation and told the court that he worked as a porter and was once a porter which was hired by William Burke.

On Saturday the 1st of November 1828, William Burke requested John M'Culloch to meet at his lodging house at 6 pm that evening. He was summoned to carry an item for him.

M'Culloch arrived on time that Saturday and as he walked through the door, he spotted William Burke placing a sheet into a box. Upon closer inspection, he noticed that when he lifted the box to carry it to the location of Burke's choice, he noticed what looked like hair. Without thinking, John M'Culloch lifted the lid slightly and placed the hair back into the box and closed it again. Upon asking if anyone was with William Burke at this time, John M'Culloch confessed that William Hare was with the men.

William Burke ordered John M'Culloch to carry the box down through Cowgate and up the High School Wynd. Burke and Helen MacDougal passed M'Culloch at High School Wynd and it was around here that William Hare and Margaret Laird met up with the couple. John M'Culloch was ordered to leave the box near the gate to 10 Surgeons Square, then he felt a form of relief flowing over him. Not long after this, William Burke ordered M'Culloch to walk to Newington with him and his friends, to go to Dr Knox's house for their payments.

After their trip to the Doctors house, they decided to go to a public house for a dram of whisky. While in the pub, a young man gave William Burke some money, then Burke paid William Hare and they both paid John M'Culloch.

John M'Culloch was asked again by the court if he was sure that the woman he saw with Burke and Hare that day was Helen MacDougal, who was sitting in the courtroom. He replied that it was and that he was also positive that they were also with Mrs Hare (Margaret Laird). With that, the court moved on to their next witness.

John Fisher

John Fisher was a local policeman in the city of Edinburgh when the case and Burke and Hare took place.

He told the court when questioned that Mr Grey was in the police station before he arrived for work at 7 o'clock. It is unknown if it was am or pm.

Fisher made his way to West Port to speak to William Burke and to see if he could physically see anything suspicious that may indicate that Mr Grey's story was true. As he entered the passage, John Fisher spotted William Burke and Helen MacDougal coming out of a neighbouring flat. The policeman spoke to the couple in their home and Fisher asked Burke what had happened to their recent lodgers. William Burke admitted that he had kicked the Greys out of their home, due to their bad conduct. To John Fisher, this seemed like a reasonable explanation and maybe the Grey's had invented the story to get even with the couple.

The next question was when the Grey's left the household, who took their place and what happened to that person? Burke had stated to Fisher that an elderly lady had spent the day and night with them, but she had been in Edinburgh to look for her son. Burke stated that the woman had left their home at 7 am on Saturday. He claimed that William Hare had seen the old woman walk away.

John Fisher had a quick look around their lodging house and he spotted a couple of spots of blood on the bed or bedding. Helen MacDougal claimed that a woman had laid in that spot a couple of weeks ago and the sheets and room had not been washed since. When Fisher spoke to MacDougal out of earshot of William Burke, she claimed that the elderly woman in question lived in Pleasence and would be found nearby to where she lived. MacDougal also stated that she had seen the woman after she had left the lodging house. The woman had approached Helen MacDougal and apologised for her behaviour when she stayed with the couple. John Fisher then asked Helen MacDougal what time the lady left the lodging house. Helen MacDougal stated the woman had been a nuisance, so she had kicked her out of the house at 7 pm on Friday. From speaking to William Burke and Helen MacDougal separately, John Fisher realised that the times did not add up and found their stories completely separate. He escorted both Burke and MacDougal to the station where he stated that he needed to question them further.

While at the station, John Fisher told the court, that he spoke to his superintendent and told him that he had found blood in Burke's room. That evening while William Burke and Helen MacDougal were still in custody, John Fisher, Dr Black and the superintendent visited Burke's lodging house to do a more detailed examination. When they arrived Burke's neighbour Mrs Law, came into the room to assist them. Together they found a red striped nightdress which was worn by the woman. The nightclothes were taken to the police station. Unfortunately, apart from the blood, this was the only evidence that they had found.

The following morning Fisher and Paterson went to see Dr Knox in Surgeon's Square and was shown the body of a naked deceased woman, Mr Grey was sent for to identify the remains. He recognised the woman immediately. That day the body was removed from Surgeon's Square and taken to the police station, where it was identified by Mrs Conway.

John Fisher voiced to the court that when the officers approached William Burke, Helen MacDougal, William Hare and Margaret Laird, they all denied knowledge of the body.

William Hare

William Hare was the main witness in the case and was next to enter the stand, being sworn in by Lord Meadowbank. Hare had turned King's evidence again his co-conspirator and agreed to incriminate William Burke, so he could be let off for his crime. It is unknown what William Burke made of this questioning or if he knew that his friend had turned against him.

Lord Meadowbank began speaking to William Hare and explained that it was in his best interests to answer the questions with the truth. Hare agreed that he would.

When beginning to be asked the question that would give his friend the death penalty, William Hare told the court that he was born in Ireland and had been living in Scotland for the past ten years. He admitted that he followed the Catholic religion, so the court asked how he would like to be sworn into court. Hare stated that he did not have a preference, so the New Testament was used.

William Hare claimed that he had known William Burke for around a year. At the time of meeting Burke, he had met Helen MacDougal, who was already co-habiting with Burke.

On the 31st of October, William Hare was in a public house drinking with a man named 'Rymer' (could this be the Rymer that owned the shop?) After that, they began drinking with William Burke. When asked by Lord Meadowbank, how much he had drunk that day, Hare stated that he drank a 'gill' by 4 pm.

Gill – *A Gill of whisky measures approximately a quarter of a pint.*

William Hare told the courtroom that, that morning he had known that William Burke was in the presence of a woman and Burke had taken her to his house. William Burke told William Hare that 'he would have a shot for the doctor'. When questioned Hare admitted that he understood Burke's comment and that it meant that he would be murdering the woman. However, when asked Hare stated that he did not go seek help for the poor lady or attempt to stop William Burke.

When William Hare entered Burke's home during the day on Friday, he found the elderly woman washing her gown in the company of Helen MacDougal. Lord Meadowbank asked William Hare to describe the gown to the court and Hare mentioned that it was red and stripy. He then pointed to the gown which was in police evidence and asked if this was the clothing that he was referring to and Hare agreed that it was.

William Hare did not stay at the house long and left around five minutes after he entered. He then made his way home.

That evening in had been in the company of Mr and Mrs Conway, in Conway's home, which was near to Burke's lodging house. While inside he was speaking to John Conway, William Burke and John Brogan. There was another man inside the house but he did not know him by name. While at the Conway's the drinks began to flow as the men's partners and the elderly woman were talking to one another.

Fast forward a few hours and just before midnight William Hare and Margaret Laird walked around to William Burke's house for a drink at the request of Helen MacDougal. When they entered the home, they spotted the elderly woman and John Brogan sitting by the fire. The group began to drink even more. When Hare walked in, William Burke asked what he was doing there and Hare told him that Helen MacDougal had invited them around to the house for a dram. After this comment, William Burke lifted his fist and hit William Hare. This led to the two men fighting in a drunken fuelled haze. Margaret Laird and Helen MacDougal attempted to break up the fight but this seemed to have unsettled the elderly woman, who then made her way to the front door screaming murder or help. After Helen MacDougal saw what she was doing she ran over to the woman and brought her back into the house and attempted to calm her down. This happened at least twice during the short fight.

While the men were fighting, William Burke managed to push William Hare onto the bed, as he got up and the fighting continued, William Hare accidentally knocked the elderly woman off the stool that she was sitting on and onto the floor. The woman who had also been drinking partially sat up and began to shout at the men. This seemed to have stopped them from fighting and as soon as they did, William Burke walked over to the woman and threw himself on top of her and began to suffocate her. He placed one of his hands under her nose and then placed the other hand under her chin. She tried to cry out but eventually made no noise at all. During the ten to fifteen minutes that it took for the woman to die, William Hare claimed that he sat on the wooden stool watching William Burke. Hare claimed that Burke did not say anything during this period and when he was satisfied that the woman was dead, he stripped her of her clothes and stashed the items away under his bed. He then moved the elderly woman's remains next to the bottom of the bed and placed a sheet on top of her and got some rope to tie her head to her feet. He then covered her with straw.

William Hare declared while all this was going on, Margaret Laird and Helen MacDougal ran outside into the passage and did not re-enter the building until the body was covered up by the straw. However, no one attempted to get help for the lady or try to pull Burke off the woman. As soon as the ordeal was over with William Burke walked out of his house, returning around ten minutes later with Mr Jones. No one in the household mentioned Margaret Docherty that night.

Mr Jones lived across the main street at West Port. William Burke had asked Mr Jones to look at the body and asked him to get a box that is big enough to fit the body inside. Mr Jones refused to look in the direction that Burke was pointing. It was at this time that Helen MacDougal and Margaret Laird were both laid in bed near to where the body was situated. It is not known if the woman were asleep or awake during this time.

William Hare admitted that while sitting on the stool which was placed next to the bed, he fell asleep with his head resting on the bed, while John Brogan joined the two women on the bed. When Hare woke between 6 and 7 am, he said the women and Brogan were still laying on the bed. When Margaret Laird woke, William Hare and Laird went home.

Back at Tanner's Close, Mr and Mrs Hare saw the Grey family, who had been lodging at their house the night before. William Hare claimed the Grey's had fallen out with William Burke the day before, so they left their home and had approached Margaret Laird for a bed.

Shortly after William Hare met William Burke at Rymer's shop. There they drank a gill of whisky together. Hare claimed that Burke had asked his friend if he would occupancy him to Surgeon's Square to enquire about a box.

The men made their way through Grassmarket, to Surgeon's Square in an attempt to speak to Dr Knox, but they did not manage to get a box, so they headed back to West Port. Again, they went into Rymer's Shop where William Burke brought a box and it was brought to his house by a porter. Hare arrived back to the house alone, followed by William Burke and an unknown male approximately a quarter of an hour later. The killers placed the body of the elderly woman into the box, along with the sheet that covered her still tied up body. By tying the body up, it had made it easier to place inside the box. The other man which was in the room then took the box away and carried it to Surgeon's Square. The men had decided beforehand to make the exchange as quickly as possible. To allow this to happen, William Hare told the court, that he walked with the porter, while William Burke went to see Dr Knox's assistant. They would all meet up again at Surgeon's Square, along with their partners Helen MacDougal and Margaret Laird.

While the women stayed out of the way, the men took their box inside 10 Surgeons Square and put the remains in the cellar. With Dr Knox not being around that day, they were told by the assistant to walk to Newington to collect their money along with his assistant 'Paterson'. When they arrived, the assistant gave William Burke five pounds and asked him to collect the rest the following day. After this William Hare claimed that he carried on his day as normal.

During Hare's interrogation by Mr Cockburn, Hare told him that he had been in

Edinburgh for ten years. During this time, he had worked as a labourer and on a boat in the Union Canal. At some point (date unknown), Hare had sold Fish out of a cart to the people that were living in the city.

When asked about him collecting money from Dr Knox, Hare stated that he had never been given any money from the Doctor or his assistant. If he did receive any money, it was from the hands of William Burke. He went on further and claimed that all of the money went from Dr Knox to William Burke.

The subject moved on to the event when Hare had knocked the elderly lady over during the night of the 31st of October. Again, William Hare admitted that the lady was alive and well and he knew this because of her shouting. During the minutes of suffocation, Hare claimed that noises that came from the woman's mouth, were not loud and after that, he heard her moaning.

William Hare confessed to the court, that while William Burke was ending this woman's life, he was sitting on the stool and the women were outside. He then confirmed that he did not attempt to shout or to seek help for the woman, neither did he go to the police the following day.

Mrs Hare (Margaret Laird)

Margaret Hare (Laird) told the court that the Grey family had slept in her home on Friday 31st October because William Burke had asked her to put them up for the night.

Between 8 and 9 pm that evening, Margaret Laird went out to look for her husband William Hare. She found him at Mrs Conway's house. Hare was talking to John Conway and William Burke at the time. Also in the house was Mrs Conway and Helen

MacDougal. The people in the Conway's at the time were drinking whisky, while in the presence of an elderly woman, which had come along with William Burke.

Burke, Hare, their wives and the old women then went back to William Burke's house. Margaret Laird claimed that after a while a fight had broken out between William Burke and William Hare. Laird stated that she had attempted to break up the fight, while Helen MacDougal claimed the elderly woman down. Margaret Laird then admitted that the woman was indeed pushed down to the ground, however, she could not say who had pushed her.

She told the court, that when it was clear that William Burke was attempting to take the life of the elderly woman, she and Helen MacDougal ran outside into the passage. She exclaimed that she did not hear any noise coming from the woman and it was the final time that she had saw the elderly woman before she had left the room.

As Margaret Laird re-entered the house, she then fell asleep on the bed. The following day, Laird had collected a box from Rymer's shop and a porter named M'Culloch took the heavy box to Surgeons Square. Laird admitted that she had followed M'Culloch with her husband William Hare.

It seems that Margaret Laird did not speak to anyone about what happened in William Burke's house that night and neither did Helen McDougal. However, when they did speak with one another, the women were unnerved thinking that the men may turn on them next. Mrs Hare claimed that she had already left her husband three times before, due to the breakdown in their relationship and feared that if she left him again, their female neighbours (mainly Mrs Law and Mrs Conway) would not assist her again.

Mr Black

Mr Black worked as a surgeon in Edinburgh. He was sworn into court by Lord Mackenzie. He explained to the court that he was shown the remains of an elderly woman on Sunday the 2nd of November at the Police Station. He made an external examination of the woman and admitted that he could not find any bruising or markings on her body to show how she had died. There were no wounds, cuts or scratches either. However, what Mr Black did find was some blood around the nostril area. But considerable time had passed before he was able to view the body. This decomposition had slightly changed the appearance of the woman. She was now swollen and her eye colour had a darker tint to them.

Medically Mr Black claimed, he could not find a cause of death for the woman, however, in his personal opinion, Mr Black stated that he thought that she could have been suffocated by her lungs and chest being pressed down.

When Black was cross-examined, he admitted that he had seen many cases like this in his career and their cause of death was caused by suffocation and all these cases were similar to the elderly woman.

Dr Christison

Dr Christison worked as a Pathologist in Edinburgh. When he spoke to the court, he told them that he had examined the body of Margaret Docherty at the Police Station on Sunday the 2nd of November. Helping him with this task was a man named Mr Newbigging. Christison told the court after his examination, he went back the following day to look over the body once more.

Upon his inspection of the woman's body, he claimed that he had found several contusions on the body. Some were seen on the legs, left shoulder blade, upper lip and two which could be seen on her head.

Unlike Mr Black, Dr Christison examined the remains internally as well as externally. Christison claimed that he found that the ligaments in the neck were torn and around it was internal bleeding. She also had signs of liver disorder. However, when he looked at her externally, like Mr Black there were no obvious signs of death. In the elderly woman's stomach, Christison found half-digested porridge, but could not tell the court if she had drunk any alcohol that evening. However, he admitted that if she did drink, he would have likely smelt it, but he did not.

When the court asked Dr Christison, if he thought that the wounds were produced before or after death, Christison claimed that it had to have been before because the contusions would not appear if death had already taken place. Dr Christison's opinion was that the elderly woman had passed away from suspected suffocation and that she was most likely throttled. He told the court that this meant that one hand was placed under her chin and pressure was made upwards towards the head.

The Verdict

It was the following day on the 25th of December 1898, that the Jury retired to come up with a verdict to the case at 7.40 am. The trial lasted nearly a whole twenty-four hours.

Early that morning, the jury gathered in a separate room and took only fifty minutes to reach a verdict. Upon returning to the courtroom at 8.30 am. The chancellor stood up and read out the much earned for verdict;

*"The Jury find the Pannel, William Burke, Guilty of the third '
charge in the Indictment; and find the Indictment not Proven '
against the Pannel, for Helen MacDougal".*

Historians and researchers claim that at this time, William Burke turned around to Helen MacDougal and stated that he was relieved that she was in the clear, by saying "Nelly, you are out of the scrape."

*Not Proven - 'Not proven' was originally an experiment by the
Scottish system where juries delivered findings on individual
factual allegations rather than general verdicts as they did
previously, and as they do today.
When the experiment was abandoned, 'not proven' started to be
used as a general verdict.
Scottish law is based on the understanding that the accused is
innocent until proven guilty. Therefore, the onus is on the Crown
to prove guilt beyond all reasonable doubt".*

Berlowrahman.scot

Lord Meadowbank then addressed the Lords and the Lord Justice Clerk in front of the courtroom. He asked the Lords to take into consideration the witnesses and the immoral crime that William Burke had committed.

Finally, the time that the whole of Edinburgh had been waiting for. The Lord Justice Clerk announced his verdict on what would happen to William Burke, he stated;

"William Burke, you now stand convicted, by the verdict of a most respectable Jury of your country, of the atrocious murder charged against you in this indictment, upon evidence which carried conviction to the mind of every man that heard it, in establishing your guilt of that offence. I agree so completely with my brother on my right hand, who has so fully and eloquently described the nature of your offence, that I will not occupy the time of the Court in commenting on it, farther than by saying, that one of a blacker description, — more atrocious in point of cool-blooded deliberation, and systematic arrangement, and where the motives were so comparatively base. — never was exhibited in the annals of this, or -of any other Court of Justice. I have no intention, Sir, to detain this audience, by repeating what has been so well expressed by my brother. My duty is of a different nature; for if ever it was clear, beyond all possibility of a doubt, that the sentence of a Criminal Court will be carried into execution, in any case, yours is that one, — and you may rest assured, that you have now no other duty to perform on earth, but to prepare, in the most suitable manner, for appearing before the Throne of Almighty God, to answer for this crime, and for every other that you have been guilty of during your life. The necessity of repressing offences of this most extraordinary and alarming description, precludes the possibility of your entertaining the slightest hope that there will be any alteration upon your sentence. In regard to your case, the only doubt that has come across my mind, is, whether, in order to mark the sense that the Court entertains of your offence, and which the violated laws of the country entertain respecting it, your body should not be exhibited in chains, in order

to deter others from the like crimes in time coming. But, taking into consideration that the public eye would be offended with so dismal an exhibition, I am disposed to agree that your sentence shall be put in execution in the usual way, but accompanied with the statutory attendant of the punishment of the crime of murder. That your body should be publicly dissected and anatomized. And I trust, that if it is ever customary to preserve skeletons, yours will be preserved, in order that posterity may keep in remembrance your atrocious crimes. I would entreat you to betake yourself immediately to a thorough repentance, and to humble yourself in the sight of Almighty God. — Call instantly to your aid the ministers of religion, of whatever persuasion you are, — avail yourself, from this hour forward, of their instructions; so that you may be brought, in a suitable manner, urgently to implore pardon from an offended God. I need not allude to any other case than what has occupied our attention these many hours; you are conscious in your own mind, whether the other charges that were exhibited against you yesterday morning, were such as might be established against you or not; — I refer to them, merely for the purpose of again recommending that you may devote the few days that you are on earth, to imploring forgiveness from Almighty God".

Lord Justice Clerk (1898)

The Lord Justice Clerk told the court that he would be jailed until his execution date on the 28th of January 1929, where he would only be fed bread and water. He announced that on this date, William Burke would be taken to Lawnmarket where he would be hanged until dead between 8 am and 10 am, after his, his body will be transported to Dr Alexander Monro, who would dissect it and persevere his skeleton.

He then went on to address Helen MacDougal. The Lord Justice Clerk stated that there was not enough proof if she assisted with these crimes and only, she will know if she did. He advised her to find a new path in life to the one that she had been leading down for the past few years. Helen MacDougal was then dismissed from the courtroom and William Burke was led back to his cell to await death.

THE CONFESSIONS

While waiting for his death sentence to arrive, William Burke must have been doing some deep thinking. It is unknown if he now knew that he was taking the wrap for William Hare's crimes. Would Burke have been happy to take the fall for his friend? At the time of the trial, William Hare was only 21 years old, whilst William Burke was a sickly 36-year-old man. It makes you wonder if William Burke decided to take the blame because he knew that he was of ill health and with that, he was addicted to laudanum to try to ease his pain.

Time in the cell must have passed by slowly for William Burke. He returned to his religious routes and asked for the forgiveness of God. A Catholic priest visited him on a few occasions to assist Burke in dealing with what he and William Hare had done. Forgiveness, comfort and confession must have occurred in his dark cell. As the days went by, William Burke's health began to decline further. As stated at the trial he was to be fed only solely on bread and water, however, his diet had to be changed so that the officers could keep him alive to be able to carry out his execution.

With all lost and nothing else to lose, William Burke gave at least two confessions from his cell. The confessions that are written in this book are printing in the same way that they were originally written. The first one was given to the local officers and detailed his crimes:

L.A Mackay

Confession Of William Burke In His Jail Cell

3rd January 1829, Edinburgh

Present—Mr. George Tait, Sheriff-substitute; Air. Archibald Scott, Procurator fiscal; Mr Richard J. Moxey, Assistant Sheriff-clerk.

Compared William Burke, at present under sentence of death in the jail of Edinburgh, states that he never saw Hare till the Hallow-fair before last (November 1827), when he and Helen McDougal met Hare's wife, with whom he was previously acquainted, on the street; they had a dram, and he mentioned he had an intention to go to the west country to endeavour to get employment as a cobbler ; but Hare's wife suggested that they had a small room in their house which might suit him and McDougal, and that he might follow his trade of a cobbler in Edinburgh ; and he went to Hare's house, and continued to live there, and got employment as a cobbler. An old pensioner, named Donald, lived in the house about Christmas, 1827

He was in bad health, and died a short time before his quarter's pension was due: that he owed Hare £4; and a day or two after the pensioner's death, Hare proposed that his body should be sold to the doctors, and that the declarant should get a share of the price. Declarant said it would be impossible to do it, because the man would be coming in with the coffin immediately; but after the body was put into the coffin and the lid was nailed down, Hare started the lid with a chisel, and he and declarant took out the corpse and concealed it in the bed, and put tanner's bark from behind the house into the coffin, and covered it with a sheet, and nailed down the lid of the coffin, and the coffin was then carried away for interment. That Hare did not appear to have been concerned in any thing of the kind before, and seemed to be at a loss how to get the body disposed of; and he and Hare went in the evening to the yard of the College, and saw a person like a student there, and the declarant asked him if there were any of Dr. Monro's men about, because he did not know there was any other way of disposing of a dead body—nor did Hare. The young man asked what they wanted with Dr. Monro, and the declarant told him that he had a subject to dispose of, and the young man referred him to Dr. Knox, No. 10 Surgeon Square; and they went there, and saw young gentlemen, whom he now knows to be Jones, Miller, and Ferguson, and told them that they had a subject to dispose of, but they did not ask how they had obtained it; and they told the declarant and Hare to come back when it was dark, and that they themselves would find a porter to carry it. Declarant and Hare went home and put the body into a sack, and carried it to Surgeon Square, and not knowing how to dispose of it, laid it down at the door of the cellar, and went up to the room, where the three young men saw them, and told them to bring up the body to the room, which they did; and they took the body out of the sack, and laid it on the dissecting-table. That the shirt was on the body, but the young men asked no questions as to that; and the declarant and Hare, at their desire, took off the shirt, and got £7 10s. Dr. Knox came in after the shirt was taken off, and looked at the body, and proposed they should get £7 10s., and authorised Jones to settle with them; and he asked no questions as to how the body had been obtained. Hare got £4 5s. and the declarant got £3 5s. Jones, &c., said that they would be glad to see them again when they had any other body to dispose of. Early last spring, 1828, a woman from Gilmerton came to Hare's house as a nightly lodger,—Hare keeping seven beds for lodgers : That she was a stranger, and she and Hare became merry, and drank together; and next morning she was very ill in consequence of what she had got, and she sent for more drink, and she and Hare drank together, and she became very sick and vomited ; ar. J at that time she had not risen from bed, and Hare then said that they would try and smother her in order to dispose of her body ' o the doctors. That she was lying on her back in the bed, and quite insensible from drink, and Hare clapped his hand on her mouth and nose, and the declarant laid himself across her body, in order to prevent her making any disturbance— and she never stirred ; and they took her out of bed and undressed her, and put her into a chest; and they mentioned to Dr. Knox's young men that they had another subject, and Mr. Miller sent a porter to meet them in the evening at the back of the Castle ; and declarant and Hare carried the chest till they met the porter, and they accompanied the porter with the chest to Dr. Knox's class-room, and Dr. Knox came in when they were there: the body was cold and stiff. Dr. Knox approved of its being so fresh, but did not ask any questions.

The next was a man named Joseph, t a miller who had been lying badly in the house: That he got some drink from declarant and Hare, but was not tipsy: he was very ill, lying in bed, and could not speak sometimes, and there was a report on that account that there was fever in the house, which made Hare and his wife uneasy in case it should keep away lodgers, and they (declarant and Hare) agreed that they should suffocate him for the same purpose; and the declarant got a small pillow and laid it across Joseph's mouth, and Hare lay across the body to keep down the arms and legs ; and he was disposed of in the same manner, to the same persons, and the body was carried by the porter who carried the last body.

In May, 1828, as he thinks, an old woman came to the house as a lodger, and she was the worse of drink, and she got more drink of her own accord, and she became very drunk, and declarant suffocated her; and Hare was not in the house at the time; and she was disposed of in the same manner.

Soon afterwards an Englishman lodged there for some nights, and was ill of the jaundice: that he was in bed very unwell, and Hare and declarant got above him and *held him down, and by holding his mouth suffocated him, and disposed of him in the same manner.*

Shortly afterwards an old woman named Haldane, (but he knows nothing farther of her) lodged in the house, and she had got some drink at the time, and got more to intoxicate her, and he and Hare suffocated her, and disposed of her in the same manner.

Soon afterwards a cinder woman came to the house as a lodger, as he believes, and she got drink from Hare and the declarant, and became tipsy, and she was half asleep, and he and Hare suffocated her, and disposed of her in the same manner. About Midsummer 1828, a woman, with her son or grandson, about twelve years of age, and who seemed to be weak in his mind, came to the house as lodgers; the woman got a dram, and when in bed asleep, he and Hare suffocated her: and the boy was sitting at the fire in the kitchen, and he and Hare took hold of him, and carried him into the room, and suffocated him. They were PUT INTO A HERON BARREL THE SAME NIGHT, AND CABRIED TO Dr. KNOX'S ROOMS.

"William Hare gave the same account as Burke of the number, and the same description of the victims; but they differ in the order of time in which the murders were committed. He stated, with great probability, that the body of Joseph, the miller, was the second sold (that of the old pensioner being the first), and, of course, he was the first man murdered. Burke, with less likelihood, asserts, as above, that the first murder was that of the female lodger. We are apt to think that Hare was right; for there was an additional motive to reconcile them to the deed in the miller's case—the fear that the apprehensions entertained through the fever would discredit the house, and the consideration that there was, as they might think, less crime in killing a man who was to die at any rate. It is not odd that Burke acted upon, as he seems always to have been,

by ardent spirits, and involved in a constant succession of murder, should have misdated the two actions".

Sir Walter Scott, Burke and Hare

That, soon afterwards, the declarant brought a woman to the house as a lodger; and after some days she got drunk, and was disposed of in the same manner: That declarant and Hare generally tried if lodgers would drink, and if they would drink, they were disposed of in that manner. The declarant then went for a few days to the house of Helen McDougal's father, and when he returned, he learned from Hare that he had disposed of a woman in the declarant's absence, in the same manner, in his house; but the declarant does not know the woman's name, or any farther particulars of the case, or whether any other person was present or knew of it.

That about this time he went to live in Broggan's house, and a woman, named Margaret Haldane, daughter of the woman Haldane before mentioned, and whose sister is married to Clark, a tinsmith in the High Street, came into the house, but the declarant does not remember for what purpose; and she got drink, and was disposed of in the same manner: That William Hare was not present, and neither John Broggan nor his son knew the least thing about that or any other case of the same kind.

That in April, 1828, he fell in with the girl Paterson and her companion in Constantine Burke's house, and they had breakfast together, and he sent for Hare, and he and Hare disposed of her in the same manner; and Mr. Ferguson and a tall lad, who seemed to have known the woman by sight, asked where they had got the body; and the declarant said he had purchased it from an old woman at the back of the Canongate. The body was disposed of five or six hours after the girl was killed, and it was cold, but not very stiff', but he does not recollect of any remarks being made about the body being warm. One day in September or October 1828, a washer-woman had been washing in the house for some time, and he and Hare suffocated her, and disposed of her in the same manner.

Soon afterwards, a woman named McDougal, who was a distant relation of Helen McDougal's first husband, came to Broggan's house to see McDougal; and after she had been coming and going to the house for a few days, she got drunk, and was served in the same way by the declarant and Hare.

That "Daft Jamie" was then disposed of in the manner mentioned in the indictment, except that Hare was concerned in it. That Hare was lying alongside of Jamie in the bed, and Hare suddenly turned on him, and put his hand on his mouth and nose; and Jamie, who had got drink, but was not drunk, made a terrible resistance, and he and Hare fell from the bed together. Hare still keeping hold of Jamie's mouth and nose; and as they lay on the floor together, declarant lay across Jamie, to prevent him from resisting, and they held him in that state till he was dead, and he was disposed of in the same manner: and Hare took a brass snuff-box and a spoon from Jamie's pocket; and kept the box to himself, and never gave it to the declarant—but he gave him the spoon.

And the last was the old woman Docherty, for whose murder he has been convicted. That she was not put to death in the manner deponed to by Hare on the trial. That during the scuffle between him and Hare, in the course of which he was nearly strangled by Hare, Docherty had crept among the straw, and after the scuffle was over, they had some drink, and after that they both went forward to where the woman was lying sleeping, and Hare went forward first, and seized her by the mouth and nose, as on former occasions; and at the same time the declarant lay across her, and she had no opportunity of making any noise ; and before she was dead, one or other of them, he does not recollect which, took hold of her by the throat. That while he and Hare -ere struggling, which was a real scuffle, McDougal opened the door of the apartment, and went into the inner passage and knocked at the door, and called out police and murder, but soon came back; and at the same time Hare's wife called out never to mind, because the declarant and Hare would not hurt one another. That whenever Le and Hare rose and went towards the straw where Docherty was lying, McDougal and Hare's wife, who, he thinks, were lying in bed at the time, or, perhaps, were at the fire, immediately rose and left the house, but did not make any noise, zero far as he heard, and he was surprised at their going out at that time, because he did not see how they could have any suspicion of what they (the declarant and Hare) intended doing. That he cannot say whether he and Hare would have killed Docherty or not, if the women had remained, because they were so determined to kill the woman, the drink being in their head; —and he has no knowledge or- suspicion of Docherty's body having been offered to any person besides Dr. Knox; and he does not suspect that Paterson would offer the body to any other person than Dr. Knox.

Declares, that suffocation was not suggested to them by any person as a mode of killing, but occurred to Hare on the first occasion before mentioned, and was continued afterwards because it was effectual, and showed no marks; and when they lay across the body at the same time, that was not suggested to them by any person, for they never spoke to any person on such a subject; and it was not done for the purpose of preventing the person from breathing, but was only done for the purpose of keeping down the person's arms and thighs, to prevent the person struggling.

Declares, that with the exception of the body of Docherty, they never took the person by the throat, and they never leapt upon them; and declares that there were no *marks of violence on any of the subjects, and they were sufficiently cold to prevent any suspicion on the part of the Doctors; and, at all events, they might be cold and stiff' enough before the box was opened up, and he and Hare always told some story of their having purchased the subjects from some relation or other person who had the means of disposing of them, about different parts of the town, and the statements which they made were such as to prevent the Doctors having any suspicions; and NO SUSPICIONS were expressed by Dr. Knox or any of his assistants, and NO QUESTIONS asked tending to show that they had suspicion.*

Declares, that Helen McDougal and Hare's wife were no way concerned in any of the murders, and neither of them knew of any thing of the kind being intended, even in the case of Docherty; and although these two women may latterly have had some suspicion in their own minds that the declarant and Hare were concerned in lifting dead bodies, he does not think they could have any suspicion that he and Hare were concerned in committing murders.

Declares, that none of the subjects which they had procured, as before mentioned, were offered to any other person than Dr. Knox's assistants, and he and Hare had very little communication with Dr. Knox himself; and declared, that he has not the smallest suspicion of any other person in this, or in any other country, except for William Hare and himself, being concerned in killing persons and offering 265Burke and Hare. their bodies for dissection; and he never knew or heard of such a thing having been done before.

Wm. Burke.

G. Tait.

Unfortunately, it seems like William Burke was not entirely happy with this confession and being able to write, he wrote another confession and asked a prison guard to hand it to the local Edinburgh newspaper after he was executed. According to Janet Philp, the officer declined the deal in fear of losing his job and where William Burke was situated was full of people who were awaiting their execution. However, there was one man who was sentenced for murder but was about to be released from jail. Philp insists that William Burke gave this man the letter and he did deliver it to the newspaper.

William Burke's handwriting

(Notice that his surname does not have an 'E' on the end)

Andrew Ewart

Andrew Ewart was born in 1786 in Midlothian, Scotland and lived at Broken Bridge in Liberton, Edinburgh with his wife Elisabeth (Nee. Tweedall) and children Andrew (1811), Alexander (1813), John (1817), George (1819), James (1822) and Euphemia (1825). He worked as a labourer.

The couple married at Liberton Kirk on the 18th of February 1811. Very soon after their wedding day, Elisabeth fell pregnant and gave birth to their son Andrew on the 11th of November that year. This was followed by five other children.

The Ewart family liked to help in the community and when men were asked to volunteer to do some night shifts at the local graveyard, Andrew Ewart agreed to help. Their job was to guard the cemetery in case of any resurrectionists turns up to dig up a grave. At certain points during the night, the group of men who were on shift would walk around the cemetery looking for any activity. In-between this time, they would keep watching out of the window in the guard tower, which looked over the graveyard and was built for this purpose.

Liberton Kirk

There is evidence that a church has been situated on this site since 1143. The church belonged to the Parish of St Cuthbert, which was granted by King David I to be built.

During a storm in the August of 1744, the church bell was struck by lightning. It took three years before the church could raise enough funds to replace it. This new bell was made by Henderson and Ormiston. After the old church was demolished in 1814, due to its decaying, the bell was transferred into the new church.

The foundation stone of the new Liberton Kirk was placed down on the 27th of January 1815 and unfortunately, we do not know when the church officially re-opened again.

In 1882, the church again was altered at the cost of £1,200. This altercation reduced the seating numbers. Again, this happened in 1958 when approximately 100 seats were taken out, due to the reduced size of the community who attended the church.

Other alterations to the building were also performed over the years. A church hall was built in 1885 and a kitchen was later added. Another hall was erected in the 1950s and this houses a tennis court and café. Today the building is still in use.

The Murder

On Tuesday 4th of December 1827 until the early hours of Wednesday 5th of December, Andrew Ewart was on resurrection duty with his friend Henry Pennycook (sometimes his surname was spelt as Pennycuick) and another man.

During the evening the men were drinking and talking to one another while watching for any activity in the graveyard. Henry Pennycook left the conversation unnoticed to go walk around the cemetery. The other men who were situated in the watch house, heard a noise coming from the cemetery. Thinking it was a gravedigger the men decided to go and investigate. As Andrew Ewart was leaving the building, he picked up a gun and followed the men out.

The men searched the grounds and Andrew Ewart spotted a dark shadow of a person in the distance. Ewart pointed the rifle at the shadow and called out a couple of times to the unknown person. Just then he heard "Surely, you'll not shoot me?" and at that moment the gun went off.

Upon inspection, it became clear that the person Andrew Ewart had shot, was his friend Henry Pennycook. Straight away, Ewart and the other men got assistance for Pennycook, who has received a bullet into his right arm. Pennycook was taken home, where a doctor attended to him. But it was no use, the wound got infected and Henry Pennycook lost his life a few days later on the 8th of December.

Unfortunately for Andrew Ewart, he was arrested for the murder of his friend, even if it was an accident. Ewart was taken to jail while awaiting his trial which occurred on the 11th of February 1828. During the short trial, Ewart was found guilty of the murder of Henry Pennycook and the jury asked the court to have mercy upon the prisoner, as he had shown regret and sympathy for what had happened.

The Lord Justice Clerk then address the courtroom and told them, that Andrew Ewart had been found guilty for a serious crime and he was given the death penalty, with his date of execution to be held on Wednesday 12th of March 1828.

It seemed like Andrew Ewart had accepted his fate, knowing that he killed one of his closest friends and understood that his life had to be taken to make it even, however, Pennycook's family did not see it that way. They believed that Ewart's sentence was too harsh and called for a re-sentence.

The National Archives holds a record for Andrew Ewart which is named Prison Records Feb 1828. The document states that Andrew Ewart was 45 years old and worked as a Labourer. He was sentenced at the High Court of Justiciary in Edinburgh on the 11th February 1828, for murder by discharging a loaded firearm at Henry Pennycook, who worked as a weaver in Liberton Churchyard on the 4th or 5th of December 1828. The document explained that Ewart was sentenced to death and to be executed until the 13th of March 1828. However, nine days after Andrew Ewart's sentence the Judge pardoned his death sentence and commuted him to a one-year prison sentence instead. It seems like a lot of people was concerned about his death sentence, this included the local people of Liberton, 182 proprietors in the area, four magistrates and Lord Provost.

Andrew Ewart was due to be released from jail in February 1829. This makes him the perfect candidate for William Burke to pass his second confession too. It is unknown if Andrew Ewart made any money for selling this confession to the paper. As for

L.A Mackay

Henry Pennycook, he was buried in Liberton Kirk and his grave still stands today.

The next pages are the courant confession in full.

The 'Courant' Confession

(From the Edinburgh Evening Courant (Newspaper), 1st February 1829)

Abigail Simpson was murdered on the 12th February 1828, on the forenoon of the day. She resided in Gilmerton, near Edinburgh; has a daughter living there. She used to sell salt and camstone (limestone). She was decoyed in by Hare and his wife on the afternoon of the 11th February, and he gave her some whisky to drink. She had one shilling and sixpence, and a can of kitchen-fee. Hare's wife gave her one shilling and sixpence for it; she drank it all with them. She then said she had a daughter. Hare said he was a single man, and would marry her, and get all the money amongst them. They then proposed to her to stay all night, which she did, as she was so drunk, she could not go home; and in the morning was vomiting. They then gave her some porter and whisky, and made her so drunk that she fell asleep on the bed. Hare then laid hold of her mouth and nose, and prevented her from breathing. Burke held her hands and feet till she was dead. She made very little resistance, and when it was convenient, they carried her to Dr. Knox's dissecting-rooms in Surgeon Square, and got ten pounds for her. She had on a drab mantle, a white grounded cotton shawl and small blue spots on it. Hare took all her clothes and went out with them; said he was going to put them into the canal. She said she was a pensioner of Sir John Hay's. (Perhaps this should be Sir John Hope.)

The next was an Englishman, a native of Cheshire, and a lodger of Hare's. They murdered him in the same manner as the other. He was ill with the jaundice at the same time. He was very tall; had black hair, brown whiskers, mixed with grey hairs. He used to sell spunks in Edinburgh; was about forty years of age. Did not know his name. Sold to Dr. Knox for £10.

The next was an old woman who lodged with Hare for one night, but does not know her name. She was murdered in the same manner as above. Sold to Dr. Knox for £10. The old woman was decoyed into the house by Mrs. Hare in the forenoon from the street when Hare was working at the boats at the canal. She gave her whisky, and put her to bed three times. At last, she was so drunk that she fell asleep and when Hare came home to his dinner, he put part of the bed-tick on her mouth and nose, and when he came home at night, she was dead. Burke at this time was mending shoes; and Hare and Burke took the clothes off her, and put her body into a tea-box. Took her to Knox's that night.

The next was Mary Paterson, who was murdered in Burke's brother's house in the Canongate, in the month of April last, by Burke and Hare, in the fore- noon. She was put into a tea-box, and carried to Dr. Knox's dissecting-rooms in the afternoon of the same day; and got £8 for her body. She had twopence HALF-PENNY, WHICH SHE HELD FAST IN HER HAND. Declares that the girl Paterson was only four hours dead till she was in Knox's dissecting-rooms, but she was not dissected at that time, for she was three months in whisky before she was dissected. She was warm when Burke cut the hair off her head; and Knox brought an artist, a painter, to look at her, she was so handsome a figure, and well-shaped in body and limbs. One of the students said she was like a girl he had seen in the Canongate as one pea is like to another. They desired Burke to cut off her hair; one of the students gave a pair of scissors for that purpose.

In June last, an old woman and a dumb boy, her grandson, from Glasgow, came to Hare's, and were both murdered at the dead hour of night, when the woman was in bed. Burke and Hare murdered her the same way as they did the others. They took off the bed-clothes and tick, stripped off her clothes, and laid her on the bottom of the bed, and then put on the bed-tick, and bed-clothes on the top of her and they then came and took the boy in their arms and carried him to the room and murdered him in the same manner, and laid him alongside of his grandmother. They lay for the space of an hour; they then put them into a herring barrel. The barrel was perfectly dry; there was no brine in it. They carried them to the stable till next day; they put the barrel into Hare's cart, and Hare's horse was yoked in it; but the horse would not drag the cart one foot past the Meal-market and they got a porter with a Hurley, and put the barrel on it. Hare and the porter went to Surgeon Square with it. Burke went before them, as he was afraid something would happen, as the horse would not draw them. When they came to Dr. Knox's dissecting-rooms, Burke carried the barrel in his arms. The students and them had hard work to get them out, being so stiff and cold. They received £16 for them both. Hare was taken in by the horse he bought that refused drawing the corpse to Surgeon Square, and they shot it in the tan-yard. He had two large holes in his shoulder stuffed with cotton, and covered over with a piece of another horse's skin to prevent them being dis- covered. Joseph, the miller by trade, and a lodger of Hare's. He had once been possessed of a good deal of money. He was connected by marriage with some of the Carron Company. Burke and Hare murdered him by pressing a pillow on his mouth and nose till he was dead. He was then carried to Dr. Knox's in Surgeon Square. They got £10 for him.

Burke and Helen McDougal were on a visit seeing their friends near Falkirk. This was at the time a procession was made round a stone in that neighbourhood thinks it was the anniversary of the battle of Bannockburn. When he was away, Hare fell in with a woman drunk in the street at the West Port. He took her into his house and murdered her himself, and sold her to Dr. Knox's assistants for £8. When Burke went away, he knew Hare was in want of money; his things were all in pawn; but when he came back, found him have plenty of money. Burke asked him if he had been doing any business, he said he had been doing nothing. Burke did not believe him, and went to Dr. Knox, who told him that Hare had brought a subject. Hare then confessed what he had done.

A cinder-gatherer; Burke thinks her name was Effy. She was in the habit of selling small pieces of leather to him (as he was a cobbler), she gathered about the coach works. He took her into Hare's stable, and gave her whisky to drink till she was drunk; she then lay down among some straw and fell asleep. They then laid a cloth over her. Burke and Hare murdered her as they did the others. She was then carried to Dr. Knox's, Surgeon Square, and sold for £10. Andrew Williamson, a policeman, and his neighbour, were dragging a drunk woman to the West Port watch-house. They found her sitting on a stair. Burke said, "Let the woman go to her lodgings." They said they did not know where she lodged. Burke then said he would take her to lodgings. They then gave her to his charge. He then took her to Hare's house. Burke and Hare murdered her that night the same way as they did the others. They carried her to Dr. Knox's in Surgeon Square, and got £10. Burke being asked, did the policemen know him when they gave him this drunk woman into his charge? He said he had a good character with the police; or if they had known that there were four murderers living in one house, they would have visited them oftener.

James Wilson, commonly called Daft Jamie. Hare's wife brought him in from the street into her house. Burke was at the time getting a dram in Rymer's shop. He saw her take Jamie off the street, bare-headed and bare-footed. After she got him into her house, and left him with Hare, she came to Rymer's shop for a pennyworth of butter, and Burke was standing at the counter. She asked him for a dram; and in drinking it she stamped him on the foot. He knew immediately what she wanted him for, and he then went after her. When in the house, she said, you have come too late, for the drink is all done; and Jamie had the cup in his hand. He had never seen him before to his knowledge. They then proposed to send for another half mutchkin, which they did, and urged him to drink; she took a little with them.

Half mutchkin – "A Scottish unit of capacity equal to a quarter of the old Scottish pint, or roughly three-quarters of an imperial pint (0.43 litres)".

Lexico.com

They then invited him ben to the little room, and advised him to sit down upon the bed. Hare's wife then went out, and locked the outer door, and put the key below the door. There were none in the room but themselves three. Jamie sat down upon the bed. He then lay down upon the bed, and Hare lay down at his back, his head raised up and resting upon his left hand. Burke was standing at the foreside of the bed. When they had lain there for some time. Hare threw his body on the top of Jamie, pressed his hand on his mouth, and held his nose with his other. Hare and him fell off the bed and struggled. Burke then held his hands and feet. They never quitted their gripe till he was dead. He never got up nor cried any. When he was dead, Hare felt his pockets, and took out a brass snuff-box and a copper snuff-spoon. He gave the spoon to Burke, and kept the box to himself. Sometime after, he said he threw the box away in the tan-yard; and the brass-box that was libelled against Burke in the Sheriff 's-office was Burke's own box. It was after breakfast Jamie was enticed in, and he was murdered by twelve o'clock in the day. Burke declares that Mrs. Hare led poor Jamie in as a dumb LAMB TO THE SLAUGHTER, AND AS A SHEEP TO THE SHEARERS; and he was always very anxious making inquiries for his mother, and was told she would be there immediately. He does not think he drank above one glass of whisky all the time. He was then put into a chest that Hare kept clothes in; and they carried him to Dr. Knox's, in Surgeon Square, that afternoon, and got £10 for him. Burke gave Daft Jamie's clothes to his brother's children; they were almost naked; and when he untied the bundle, they were like to quarrel about them. The clothes of the other murdered persons were generally destroyed, to prevent detection. Ann McDougal, a cousin of Helen McDougal's former husband. She was a young woman, and married, and had come on a visit to see them. Hare and Burke gave her whisky till she was drunk, and when in bed and asleep, Burke told Hare that he would have most to do to her, as she being a distant friend, he did not. like to begin first on her. Hare murdered her by stopping her breath, and Burke assisted him the same way as the others. One of Dr. Knox's assistants, Paterson, gave them a fine trunk to put her into. It was in the afternoon when she was done. It was in John Broggan's house; and when Broggan came home from his work he saw the trunk, and made inquiries about it, as he knew they had no trunks there. Burke then gave him two or three drams, as there- was always plenty of whisky going at these times, to make him quiet. Hare and Burke then gave him £1 10s. each, as he was back in his rent, for to pay it, and he left Edinburgh a few days after. They then carried her to Surgeon Square as soon as Broggan went out of the house, and got £10 for her. Hare was cautioner for Broggan's rent, being

£3, and Hare and Burke gave him that sum. Broggan went off in a few days, and the rent is not paid yet.

They gave him the money that he might not come against them for the murder of Ann McDougal, that he saw in the trunk, that was murdered in his house. Hare thought that the rent would fall upon him, and if he could get Burke to pay the half of it, it would be so much the better; and proposed this to Burke, and he agreed to it, as they were glad to get him out of the way. Broggan's wife is a cousin of Burke's. They thought he went to Glasgow, but are not sure. Mrs. Haldane, a stout old woman, who had a daughter transported last summer from the Calton jail for fourteen years, and has another daughter married to, in the High Street. She was a lodger of Hare's. She went into Hare's stable, the door was left open, and she being drunk, and falling asleep among some straw, 269Burke and Hare. Hare and Burke murdered her the same way as they did the others, and kept the body all night in the stable, and took her to Dr. Knox's next day. She had but one tooth in her mouth, and that was a very large one in front.

A young woman, a daughter of Mrs. Haldane, of the name of Peggy Haldane, was drunk, and sleeping in Broggan's house, was murdered by Burke himself, in the forenoon. Hare had no hand in it. She was taken to Dr. Knox's in the afternoon in a tea-box, and £8 got for her. She was so drunk at the time that he thinks she was not sensible of her death, as she made no resistance whatever. She and her mother were both lodgers of Hare's, and they were both of idle habits, and much given to drinking. This was the only murder that Burke committed by himself, but what Hare was connected with. She was laid with her face downwards, and he pressed her down, and she was soon suffocated. There was a Mrs. Hostler washing in John Broggan's, and she came back next day to finish up the clothes, and when done, Hare and Burke gave her some whisky to drink, which made her drunk. This was in the day-time. She then went to bed. Mrs. Broggan was out at the time. Hare and Burke murdered her the same way they did the others, and put her in a box, and set her in the coalhouse in the passage, and carried her off to Dr. Knox's in the afternoon of the same day, and got £8 for her. Broggan's wife was out of the house at the time the murder was committed. Mrs. Hostler had ninepence halfpenny in her hand, which they could scarcely get out of it after she was dead, so firmly was it grasped.

The woman Campbell or Docherty was murdered on the 31st October last, and she was the last one, Burke declares that Hare perjured himself on his trial, when giving his evidence against him, as the woman Campbell or Docherty lay down among some straw at the bedside, and Hare laid hold of her mouth and nose, and pressed her throat, and Burke assisted him in it, till she was dead. Hare was not sitting on a chair at the time, as he said in the Court. There were seven shillings in the woman's pocket, which were divided between Hare and Burke. That was the whole of them—sixteen in whole: nine were murdered in Hare's house, and four in John Broggans; two in Hare's stable, and one in Burke's brother's house in the Canongate. Burke declares that five of them were murdered in Hare's room that has the iron bolt in the inside of it. Burke did not know the days nor the months the different murders were committed, nor all their names. They were generally in a state of intoxication at those times, and paid little attention to them; but they were all from 12th February till 1st November, 1828; but he thinks Dr. Knox will know by the dates of paying him the money for them. He never was concerned with any other person but Hare in those matters, and was never a resurrection man, and never dealt in dead bodies but what he murdered. He was urged by Hare's wife to murder Helen McDougal, the woman he lived with. The plan was, that he was to go to the country for a few weeks, and then write to Hare that *she had died and was buried, and he was to tell this to deceive the neighbours; but he would not agree to it.*

The reason was, they COULD NOT TRUST TO HER, AS SHE WAS A SCOTCH WOMAN. Helen McDougal and Hare's wife were not present when those murders were committed: they might have a suspicion of what was doing, but did not see them done. Hare was always the most anxious about them, and could sleep well at night after committing a murder; but Burke repented often of the crime, and could not sleep without a bottle of whisky by his bedside, and a twopenny candle to burn all night beside him; when he awoke, he would take a draught of the bottle sometimes half a bottle at a draught—and that would make him sleep. They had a great many pointed out for murder, but were disappointed of them by some means or other; they were always in a drunken state when they committed those murders and when they got the money for them while it lasted. When done, they would pawn their clothes, and would take them out as soon as they got a subject. When they first began this murdering system, they always took them to Knox's after dark; but being so successful, they went in the day-time, and grew bolder. When they carried the girl Paterson to Knox's, there were a great many boys in the High School Yards, who followed Burke and the man that carried her, crying, " They are carrying a corpse " but they got her safe delivered. They often said to one another that no person could find them out, no one being present at the murders but themselves two; and that they might be as well hanged for a sheep as a lamb. They made it their business to look out for persons to decoy into their houses to murder them. Burke declares, when they kept the mouth and nose shut a very few minutes, they could make no resistance, but would convulse and make a rumbling noise in their bellies for some time; after they ceased crying and making resistance, they left them to die of themselves; but their bodies would often move afterwards, and for some time they would have long breathings before life went away. Burke declares that it was God's providence that put a stop to their murdering career, or he does not know how far

they might have gone with it, even to attack people on the streets, as they were so

successful, and ALWAYS MET WITH A READY MARKET: THAT WHEN THEY DELIVERED

A BODY THEY WERE ALWAYS TOLD TO GET MORE.

Hare was always with him when he went with a subject, and also when he got the

money. Burke declares, that Hare and him had a plan made up, that Burke and a man

were to go to Glasgow or Ireland, and try the same there, and to forward them to

Hare, and he was to give them to Dr. Knox. Hare's wife always got £1 of Burke's

share, for the use of the house, of all that were murdered in their house; for if the

price received was £10, Hare got £6, and Burke got only £4; but Burke did not give

HER THE £1 FOR DAFT JAMIE, FOR WHICH HARE'S WIFE WOULD NOT SPEAK TO HIM

FOR THREE WEEKS. They could get nothing done during the harvest-time, and also

after harvest, as Hare's house was so full of lodgers. In Hare's house were eight beds

for lodgers; they paid 3d. each; and two, and sometimes three, slept in a bed; and

during harvest they gave up their own bed when throng. Burke declares they went

under the name of resurrection men in the West Port, where they lived, but not

murderers. When they wanted money, they would say they would go and look for a

shot; that was the name they gave them when they wanted to murder any person.

They entered into a contract with Dr. Knox and his assistants that they were to get

£10 in winter, and £8 in summer for as many subjects as they could bring to them.

Old Donald, a pensioner, who lodged in Hare's house, and died of a dropsy, was the

first subject they sold. After he was put into the coffin and the lid put on. Hare

unscrewed the nails and Burke lifted the body out. Hare filled the coffin with bark

from the tan-yard, and put a sheet over the bark, and it was buried in the West

Church Yard. The coffin was furnished by the parish. Hare and Burke took him to the

College first; they saw a man there, and asked for Dr. Monro, or any of his men; the man asked what they wanted, or had they a subject; they said they had. He then ordered them to call at 10, Dr. Knox's, in Surgeon Square, and he would take it from them, which they did. They got £7 10s. for him. That was the only subject they sold that they did not murder; and getting that high price made them try the murdering for subjects.

Burke is thirty-six years of age, was born in the parish of Orrey, county Tyrone; served seven years in the army, most of that time as an officer's servant in the Donegal militia; he was married at Ballinha, in the county of Mayo, when in the army, but left his wife and two children in Ireland. She would not come to Scotland with them. He had often wrote to her, but got no answer; he came to Scotland to work at the Union Canal, and wrought there while it lasted; he resided for about two years in Peebles, and worked as a labourer. He wrought as weaver for eighteen months, and as a baker for five months; he learned to mend shoes, as a cobbler, with a man he lodged with in Leith; and he has lived with Helen McDougal about ten years, until he and she were confined in the Calton Jail, on the charge of murdering the woman of the name of Docherty or Campbell, and both were tried before the High Court of Justiciary in December last. Helen McDougal's charge was found not proven, and Burke found guilty, and sentenced to suffer death on the 28th January.

Declares, that Hare's servant girl could give information respecting the murders done in Hare's house, if she likes. She came to him at Whitsunday last, went to harvest, and returned back to him when the harvest was over. She remained until he was confined along with his wife in the Calton Jail. She then sold twenty-one of his swine for £3, and absconded. She was gathering potatoes in a field that day Daft Jamie was murdered; she saw his clothes in the house when she came home at night. Her name is Elizabeth M'Guier or Mair. Thief wives saw that people came into their houses at night, and went to bed as lodgers, but did not see them in the morning, nor did they make any inquiries after them. They certainly knew what became of them, although

Burke and Hare pretended to the contrary. Hare's wife often helped Burke and Hare to pack the murdered bodies into the boxes. Helen McDougal never did, nor saw them done; Burke never durst let her know; he used to smuggle in drink, and get better victuals unknown to her; he told her he bought dead bodies, and sold them to doctors, and that was the way they got the name of resurrection-men. " Burk declares that Doctor Knox never encouraged him, neither taught him or encouraged him to murder any person, nether any of his assistants, that worthy gentleman Mr. Ferguson was the only man that ever mentioned anything about the bodies. He inquired, where we got that young woman Paterson.

William Burk, prisoner

from Condemned Cell, January 21, 1819.

THE EXECUTION

Between the years 1800 and 1868, two hundred and seventy-three people were hanged publicly in Scotland for various crimes, this comprised of 259 men and just 14 women. A further two hundred and seven people were sentenced to be executed, however, they were reprieved at a later date.

Out of these numbers, 39 men and 3 women were convicted of murder and sentenced to death, but just 16 men and 1 woman had their sentences followed through.

Edinburgh was the second-highest area to see the most executions following the city of Glasgow with 62 executions. Edinburgh saw 59 executions between 1800 and 1869. These crimes included;

- Murder
- Robbery
- Highway Robbery
- Stouthrief (robbery of a dwelling house)
- Forgery
- Theft
- Horse Theft
- Uttering
- Rape
- Treason
- Hamesucken (seeking and invasion of a person in their home)
- Sheep Stealing
- Arson

On Tuesday the 27th of January 1829, the day before William Burke was due to be executed, he was woken in the early hours of the morning and was taken from

Carlton Hill Jail to the lock-up at Liberton's Wynd. He arrived here at approximately 4 am, under the cover of darkness without any witnesses. This move was done to attempt to protect the prisoner from the mobs of people who were wanting to get their hands on him. William Burke would spend the next day in the company of priests, while the scaffold was being erected for his personal use.

During the night, the crowds of people began to gather wherever they could. In windows, hallways, balcony's and on the ground floor. The weather was damp and cold but the locals did not care, they wanted the best seat in the house to watch the murderer die. By 7 am, a large crowd had gathered at the base of the scaffold and many windows were full of spectators, who have paid a good amount of money to get a good view of what was to come. Some witnesses from the time claimed that 20,000 to 25,000 people had gathered to see William Burke's execution.

Gold markings on the ground where Burke was executed

L.A Mackay

That morning, William Burke was given a black suit to wear for his execution, as he seemed to have taken pride in his appearance. Due to his ill health, it is more than likely that he had lost weight during his time locked up, but other than that, he looked the same.

The streets were wild, there were people selling broadside's, food and souvenirs. Many sellers made a good profit on a day like this.

It is unknown what William Burke was feeling that morning. Was he happy for it to be over or did he still want to live? Two catholic clergymen attended his cell that morning and at just before 8 am, he was assisted from Liberton's Wynd to the scaffold at Lawnmarket.

On the scaffold, William Burke shook the hands with the men that had aided him and he knelt to the ground, to say a prayer with the clergymen, while the crowd screamed pure abuse at him.

As he stood up, the executioner placed the noose over his head with the knot of the rope placed near his ear. A cotton bag was then placed over the Irish man's head so that the crowd did not have to see his expression as he dropped.

At 8 am, William Burke was hung in front of the enormous crowd. He was 36 years old.

Unfortunately, the executioner used a short rope during the hanging. This meant that Burke's neck did not snap, he was slowly strangled to death, which took between 15 to 20 minutes. All the while, the front of the crowd was attempting to get a souvenir of the day by attempting to mule his remains.

William Burke's body was dropped from the rope at 8.45 am that morning, by this time the spectators were cheering at his death and were partying like New Year's Eve.

His body was taken down and was carried over a man's shoulder to the lockup which housed William Burke before his death, then he was placed onto a cart and was transferred to Doctor Alexander Monro's surgery in the early hours of Thursday morning. By 11.30 am, any sign of an execution taking place in Lawnmarket had been removed by the workers who had erected it.

EXECUTION.

A Full and Particular account of the Execution of W. BURKE, who was hanged at Edinburgh on Wednesday the 28th January, 1829; also, an account of his conduct and behaviour since his condemnation, and on the Scaffold.

Early on Wednesday morning, the Town of Edinburgh was filled with an immense crowd of spectators, from all places of the surrounding country, to witness the execution of a Monster, whose crime stands unparalleled in the annals of Scotland : viz.—for cruelly murdering Margery M'Conegal, and afterwards selling her body to the Doctors in October last.

Whilst this unhappy man was under sentence, he made the following Confession :—that he had been engaged in this murderous traffic from Christmas, 1827, until the murder of the woman Docherty, or M'Conegal, in October last ; during which period, he had butchered Sixteen of his fellow-creatures, and that he had no accomplice but Hare,—that they perpetrated these fearful atrocities by suffocation. When they succeeded in making their victims drunk, the one held the mouth and nostrils, whilst the other went upon the body, and in this manner was the woman Docherty killed ; they then sold her body to Doctor ——— in his rooms, and received payment at his house—and that they were never Resurrectionests ; all the bodies they sold being murdered, except one, who died a natural death in Hare's house.

At an early hour on Tuesday, he was taken in a coach from the jail on the Calton-hill to the Lock-up, a prison immediately adjacent to the place of execution. He spent the day in silence, reading, and devotion, and on Tuesday night he slept soundly for several hours. About seven o'clock, the two Catholic clergymen arrived, and were admitted into the cell, and they were soon after followed by the Rev. Mr Marshall. The religious ceremonies being performed, he talked firmly, declared that death had no terrors, and expressed a hope of pardon and happiness. During the night, Burke stated that he was happy, that he had at last been arrested in his career of crime, and brought to justice. Though he had been a great offender, yet he rested on the atonement of the Saviour for salvation. When the irons were knocked off, he exclaimed, "Thank God these are off, and all will be off shortly." Shortly after eight o'clock, the procession set out for the place of execution. Bailies Crichton and Small, with a party of town officers, first ascended the scaffold, and they were followed by Burke, supported by the two Catholic Clergymen. He was dressed in decent black clothes, and was perfectly firm and composed. The moment he appeared, the crowd set up an appalling shout, which continued for several minutes. The murderer and the Catholic clergymen then knelt down and spent a few minutes in devotion, and the religious exercises were concluded by a prayer from the Rev. Mr Marshall. As soon as the executioner proceeded to do his duty, the cries of "Burke him, Burke him, give him no rope," and many others of a similar complexion, were vociferated in voices loud with indignation. Burke, in the mean time, stood perfectly unmoved, and gazed around till the cap was drawn over his face, and shut the world for ever from his view.

The executioner having completed his preparations and placed the signal in Burke's hand, the magistrates, ministers, and attendants left the scaffold. The crowd again set up another long and loud cheer, which was followed by cries for "Hare, Hare!" "Where is Hare?" "Hang Hare!" and so on. Burke lifted his hands and ejaculated a prayer of a few sentences—then dropt the napkin, and momently the drop fell. The struggle was neither long nor apparently severe; but at every convulsive motion, a loud huzza arose from the multitude, which was several times repeated even after the last agonies of humanity were past. During the time of the wretched man's suspension, not a single indication of pity was observable among the vast crowd—on the contrary, every countenance wore the lively aspect of a gala day, while puns and jokes on the occasion were freely bandied about, and produced bursts of laughter and merriment, which were not confined to the juvenile spectators alone—"Burke Hare too!" "Wash blood from the land!" "One cheer more," and similar exclamations, were repeated in different directions, until the culprit was cut down, about nine o'clock, when one general and tremendous huzza closed the awful exhibition—and the multitude immediately thereafter began to disperse.

Burke's body is to be dissected, and his Skeleton to be preserved, in order that posterity may keep in remembrance his atrocious crimes.

PRICE ONE PENNY.

Broadside about Burkes execution - digital.nls.uk

Dissection

Thursday morning William Burke's deceased body arrived at Dr Monro's theatre, where there had been a group of onlookers waiting to catch a glimpse of the hung criminal since his execution the day before. By now only a small group remained to see the delivery of the body.

When Burke arrived in the theatre, an external examination of William Burke's body was carried out by Dr Alexander Monro and other surgeons. When this was complete a death mask was made of his face in plaster. This was a common procedure with criminals and unidentified bodies that had been found.

During our research, the earliest books that were written about the case told us that William Burke was a muscular man, which a thick neck, but surprisingly had small legs and feet. The only thing that showed that Burke suffered an execution was the colouring of his neck which was a purplish tint with a rope mark. His face was normal and showed no emotion.

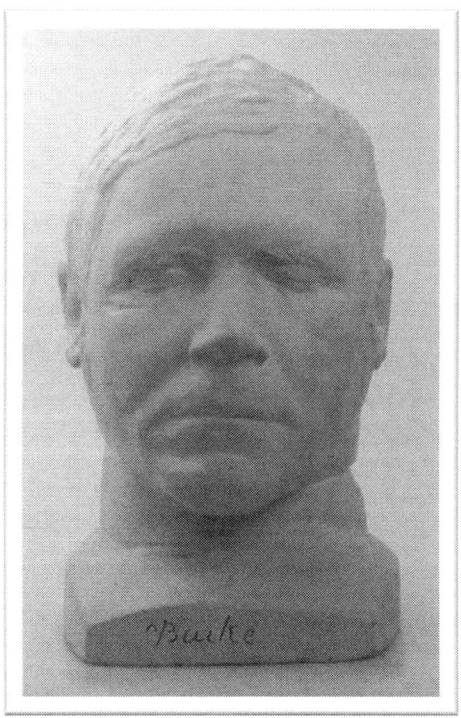

William Burke's death mask

At 1 pm that afternoon, Dr Monro began the dissection of the murderer in front of an audience, which consisted of his students, other doctors and the paying public. The room was crowded, full of spectators wanting to see Burke one final time.

When William Burke's head was open, Dr Monro took his quill pen and dipped it into his blood, he then wrote on a piece of paper;

"This is written with the blood of Wm Burke, who was hanged at Edinburgh. This blood was taken from his head".

We only have one comment about William Burke's dissection, which was written by the president of the Royal Medical Society, a man named Thomas Stone. The book named Observations on the Phrenological Development of William Burke and other atrocious murderers. This book looked at the size the criminals' skulls to see if there was any reason why they committed their crimes. In the book it states in Latin;

"Nefandi nujus homicidae cadaver explorantibus, unus tantum testiculus, quod notatu dignium est apparuit: Alter enim morbo, quo laboraverat, absorptus, prorsus fuetrat. Morbus iste testiculi evulceratio scrophulosa fuisse videtur, et ea infra posui, quae post mortem detecta fuerurrt. Scroti exterioris aspectus a sinistra quidem raphes parte naturalise erat: a dextra vero ulcera complurima, sinuosa, ut ita dicam, inertia videbantur. Haec scroti partem maxime occupabant eam, quae, corpore erecto, femori, interior apposite est, eamque etiam ubi scrotum et femur inter se continua fiunt. Alicut minus curiose inspicierti haec summae cuti tantum adjacere, neque alte ad testiculum ipsum penetrare viderentur. His tamenpatefactis, externis involucris sublates, aliquantum humoris reperiebatur coloris subflavi sive subfusci, Ei similis qui sinibus foras afflvebat. Ultra secantibus, a dextra, ne minimum quidem vestigium tunicae vaginalis, nihil testiculi appaeuit: Quorium quidem locum complebat materia quaedam semi-fluida, pulla, nullo modo peculiari olens, meconium quodammodo referens, vix tamen partier nigricans. Vesiculae seminales solito ampliores errant, humoremque subfuscum intus habebant. Pluribus in locis scroti septum exesum erat et pauxillum ideo materiae istius subatrae in sinistro quoque latere, ad partem tunicae vaginalis superiorem, et extra eam, repertum est. Eadem materia etiam refertae errant membranae, quae accelerators urinae obtegint, adiposa et callulosa. A sinistro latere, tunica vaginalis et testiculus naturali, quod ad fabrican, aspect gaudebant: hic autem testiculus certe minor erat solito, Longe aliter ac plerumque fit, ubi alter perierit testiculus. Chorda spermatica utrinque solitam superare magnitudinem inveniebatur".

Translated to English:

"Of this to see the carcass of heinous homicides, only one testicle, which is worthy to note appeared: For another disease that halted absorbed completely fuetrat. This seems to have been the testicles with the tuberculosis disease, and things below, I have laid, which took place after the death of the disclosed fururrt. Raphi was, indeed, from the left-hand side of the appearance of the exterior naturalise Scroti: on the right side, however, the ulcers are numerous and, winding, but, so to speak, the ignorance on equitable terms. This is the most important part of the nerves take possession of her, which, with the body erect, is a sign of the thigh, while the interior applied to government, and is continuous with each other, even when the wall of the scrotum and the thigh that is made. So much the less, examining the skin of HAND IN A MAN be attached to inspected these encomiums of highest, high, nor to penetrate into the testicle, they seemed to him. With these open up, the externals of the wrappings of goods, restore, or rather dark in some degree of moisture was found in the colour of the yellow, It is like the folds of outside was shaking. From beyond the they are drawn, on the right, not the least trace of the vaginal tunic, indeed, there is nothing the testicles with a appeared: A kind of a place for filling the semi-fluid or the material of which the former, and coarse, can in no special way by the odour, the meconium, in a certain sense, when he told, you will hardly find more prevalent blackish. Seminal vesicles usual baggy stray liquid inside had somewhat darker. In a small quantity of the matter was, and is, therefore, full of cavities, in many passages in the septum of the scrotum, too, were on the left side of this subatra, to a part of the upper of the vaginal tunic, and apart from that is, it was found. The same material is also full of them go astray in their membranes, which are accelerators, urine, he is covered, perirenal fat, and callulose. From the left side, and the vaginal tunic of the testicle in the natural, which to the manufactured, aspect, were glad to, but here he was, as usual, the testicle is certainly less strong, by far the other way, and for the most part *takes place, in which one of the testicles and perish. To overcome the magnitude of the vibrating string is found, usually on both sides of the spermatic".*

In recent years, many researchers claimed that William Burke was suffering from testicular cancer, however, translating these notes it becomes apparent that Burke did not have any form of cancer, but he did have sexual transmitted infections, which were slowly killing him. It is more than likely that he would have had weeks or days to live, not years. To ease the pain, William Burke probably began to take more and more laudanum and began his addiction. He probably knew by this point that there was something seriously wrong with him.

To finish the book, Thomas Stone claimed that Burke had an unusually small cranium that was found in more than one killer. Could this have been thought to be the link between criminals?

Outside the building, the crowd began to increase in size. A small fight broke out, leading to the arrival of the police, who had to calm the situation down. The crowd did not calm down without a fight. People were attempting to break into the theatre, the police had to use weapons in self-defense and the whole situation was out of control. Still, an hour and a half later, the fight continued. This stopped when a professor at the school, came out of the building and told the crowd that if they behaved, fifty people from the crowd would get the chance to see the body of William Burke after the dissection had taken place. It was as if someone had taken out a gun and everyone stopped in their tracks. It is claimed that during the fight many policemen were hurt and several of the crowd was placed into a room inside the building to await arrest.

By Friday morning, the professor had arranged for public viewing of Burke's body. This of course was to be paid for; however, it did not stop thousands of people queuing up to see the dissected male, which had been attempted to be placed back together. Basically, the viewers came in one door into the theatre, saw Burke laid out upon a table and walked out of another door. The viewing lasted until sunset that day. It is claimed that 60 people per minute walked past the corpse with mixed feelings, but it seemed that curiosity had got the better of them.

The day after the full dissection had been taking place, bearing William Burke down to just a skeleton, which was transferred and can be still seen in the museum of anatomy in Edinburgh.

Some of William Burke's skin was taken or stolen and was made into book bindings and cases. One famous book was a pocketbook which is on display in the Surgeons' Hall Museum, along with his death mask. This is more than likely why the case is still known today.

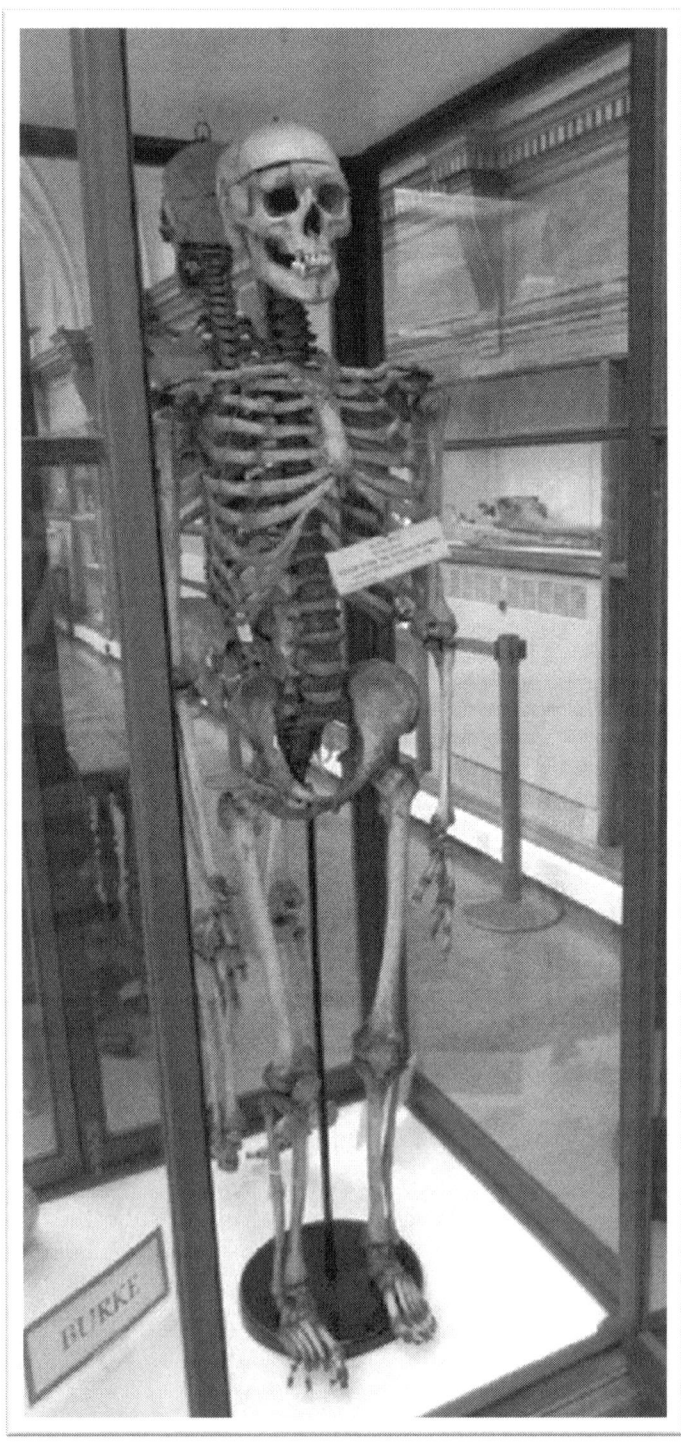

William Burke's skeleton – Researchgate.net

LIFE GOES ON

The final chapter of this book will focus on what happened to the other people in the story. Unfortunately, most of the stories that we are going to share, have not been verified by anyone. You will need to think for yourself to see if you believe any of these are accurate or did likely happen.

What happened to William Hare?

As William Burke and Helen MacDougal were only prosecuted for one of the three crimes against their victims, the family of James Wilson approached the court and asked if Hare could be placed on trial for James' murder. It was deemed that 4 out of the 6 people in court, decided that they could not go against the King's Evidence, so William Hare was free. This led the people of Edinburgh to fall out with the system.

On Thursday the 5th of February 1829, William Hare was released from Calton Gaol. This was a week after his friend William Burke's execution. The police deemed that it was not fit for the criminal to be released due to the commotion of the crimes and the groups of people who hovered around dying down.

Before he was escorted out of the building Hare was given a long heavy coat to wear and a hat, which he used to cover his face. He was escorted to Newington, where an officer placed him on a mail coach, which would go to England. The small coach was full of people who were heading out of town. William Hare opted to ride on top of the coach, however, during the journey, it began to rain and being at the beginning of February it was very cold, so he decided to sit downstairs where he had shelter. Unfortunately, also travelling on the mail coach was the lawyer for the Wilson family, who immediately recognised Hare and did not keep his identity a secret.

When the mail coach stopped at Dumfries, the passengers entered a local public house to warm up. Soon word spread about who the mysterious person was and a gang of people formed to seek justice for the victims of his crimes.

Hare decided to leave the public house to get back onto the mail coach, however, he was refused entry, leaving him out in the cold night. The people of Dumfries flew into a rage and began chasing Hare. William Hare ran into the Kings Arms Public House, where the police were notified. By now a crowd of hundreds of people were gathered outside waiting to lynch the murderer. Again, the police officer escorted William Hare to a mail coach, where he began to head away from Scotland. This is the last verified sighting of William Hare.

Author Dudley-Edwards claimed that when William Hare left Dumfries, he was spotted twice in Carlisle. The first sighting was just two hours after the officers had released him from Dumfries, which would have been very unlikely, given the distance.

Many researchers in the past have claimed that William Hare eventually made it down to London, England, where he found a job working in a lime pit. Unfortunately, after an incident, Hare ended up being blinded at work and could not work. This meant he lost his job and his home. He ended up homeless and begging the people of London for money. From other researchers that in the past have looked into the records, it appears that the blind beggar was a man named Thomas Ware. This is to not say that Hare did not change his name.

Another story of the whereabouts of William Hare which is interesting is that he did not leave Scotland. From Dumfries, he travelled north to a place called Applecross and was living by the name of William Maxwell. Looking into the genealogy of

Maxwell's life, he claimed in the census' that he was born at sea on the Atlantic Ocean around 1806 and in the 1851 and 1861 census', show that he married a woman named Mary Maitland between 1835 and 1842. Together they had four children; Flora, John, Maria and William. In the documents, it claimed that Maxwell worked as a Hand Loom Weaver.

Applecross

Applecross is situated on the mainland of Scotland, directly across from the isle of Skye. It is claimed to be a remote area of Scotland, which had been inhabited since the year 673 when a Christian settlement was formed.

A monastery was built in the area, which survived for one hundred and twenty years. However, all that remains of the monastery today disappeared years ago. In place stands a church with a graveyard.

According to Applecross.org, in 1850, 3,000 people were living in the local area. Many of the families lived on farms and cultivated their crops to live on. Today only 300 people are living in Applecross, with many of the families surviving on tourism.

In 1975, a coastal road to Applecross was built, which allowed visitors east access to visit the area.

According to the website scotsclan.com, it is claimed that several official people came to the Applecross area to look for Hare but never approached Maxwell, but it was clear that people were watching him. The website also said that Maxwell had the same deformities as William Hare, however, it does not state what they were. Maybe William Hare thought that the last place people would look for him was the north of Scotland, where he could live a quiet life.

Another theory is that William Hare had made his way back to Ireland where a retired genealogist named Shaun Cheyne, claimed that he arrived back in County Louth in 1829, where he ended his life living in a Kilkeel Workhouse, where he passed away and is buried in the grounds. However, in some documents, his surname was written as O'Hare. Cheyne also claimed that Hare's parents were named Anne and Patrick and he was born in Money Quin, which is situated near Armagh. He is also insistent that Hare had a son William, who was born in Edinburgh with Margaret Laird. Unfortunately, this theory cannot be proven.

The final theory that we want to talk about is about William Hare making his way over to Ontario, Canada. Upon travelled through Ekfrid on a coach with another person. A man who was originally from Scotland and worked under the supervision of Dr Knox began talking to another resident. Together they spoke of the Burke and Hare killings and the man told the stranger what exactly happened. This man would become a local Doctor in the town.

Rewind a few years, the Canadian native told the Doctor that a man and wife arrived in town under the surname of Hare. The couple kept out of the local's way and built a house away from the rest. This seemed to have put some interest into the Doctor.

As more English and Scottish natives arrived in Canada, a man arrived with a broadside of the Burke and Hare event. As this was 'new news' to the local people, they took it in turns to read the description of events and they began to wonder if the man Hare was William Hare, who had helped William Burke kill all of their victims. It was from then on, that Hare and his wife were ignored by the people in the town and were made to feel unwelcome. Finally having enough of the ignorant people, someone confessed to Hare when asked about the broadside. Hare approached the man who had brought it over to Canada and asked politely to read it. The man gave Hare the paper and he took it back to his house to read. As he was reading through the article, it seemed that Hare began to convulse and fall to the ground. He demanded that his wife go get a priest but it was too late, he had passed away before she could return. The only thing unusual about this story is that Hare told people that he was Christian and in his hour of need, he asked for a Catholic Priest. The same religion that William Hare was. Would he have confessed to his true identity?

There are other stories of William Hare's whereabouts that have crept up in books throughout the year. But none as much information as the stories above.

What happened to Helen MacDougal?

Helen MacDougal was released from jail on the evening of the 26th of December 1829. She was let out onto the streets of Edinburgh.

MacDougal decided to go back to her home, where she had found that it had been trashed by treasure hunters, who were wanting souvenirs of the criminals. She spent the cold night in her home, all alone, away from prying eyes. The next morning, Helen MacDougal visited her local shop, in an attempt to buy some whisky. She was instantaneously recognised and was refused and sent away. By now, the word in West Port was spreading that she had been released and was back in the area. The local people raged at the thought and gangs of people began looking for her. Helen MacDougal was saved by the police when they turned up and took her to the nearest watch house. The gang of residence, turned into an angry mob, who was wanting to see her blood. However, the policemen came up with a plan. One of the officers went outside and spoke to the people and claimed that they were holding Helen MacDougal, to collect evidence to prosecute William Hare. Upon hearing this, the locals agreed that it was a good thing and slowly went back to doing their everyday activities. However, this was a ploy. The officers then dressed MacDougal in men outer clothing and she was told to climb out of the back window and simply walk away and she did.

Helen MacDougal did not leave Edinburgh at that time. It seems that she approached William Burke's brother Constantine. Together on Tuesday the 30th of December, they walked up to the Carlton Gaol and asked to speak to William Burke. Of course, they were refused, but for good measure, Burke was told of their arrival. He passed over some money to give to them, as well as his pocket watch. This would be the final time that either of them had communicated with William Burke and this was the last known sighting of Helen MacDougal.

It is thought within the next few days, that Helen MacDougal decided to leave the city, to avoid being attacked. One theory which is written on a broadside and was published on the 25th of April 1829 in Glasgow stated that MacDougal returned to her family home in Redding, only to run out by a local mob. She then attempted to live in different places throughout Scotland, but her identity was always disclosed. She then took up with a man, who was born in Perth and together they moved to Deanston, where he found a job at Deanston Mills, which was a local cotton factory.

The couple had not been there three days when her identity was found out. Helen MacDougal was attacked by the local mob, consisting of mostly women. She is said to have been stood on, with feet pressing down on her neck and chest until there was barely any life left in her. In the crowd, there must have been some people who pitied MacDougal because they took her to a local house, where a doctor was summoned, however, it was too late. She died a few minutes later.

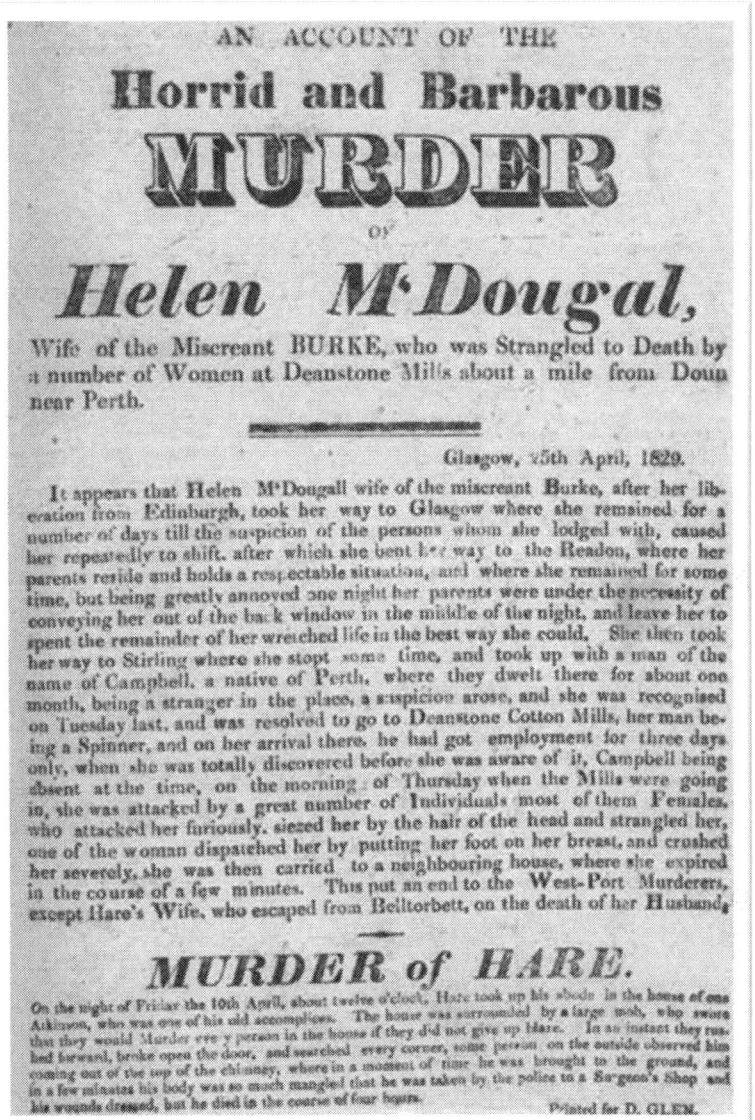

Broadside about the death of MacDougal - digital.nls.uk

Deanston Mill

To the south of River Teith, lays a small village named Deanston. Originally named

Deans Town after a man named Walter Drummond, who was the Dean of Dunblane

in the 1500s.

L.A Mackay

Before 1785, Deanston was unheard of. A cotton spinning mill named Adelphi was built around this time, however, it became clear to the developers and the Buchanan brothers, who owned the mill, that the closest accommodation was in the village of Doune, which is the nearest town. It was decided that houses would be built next to the mill, for the use of the mill workers.

Houses for mill workers in Deanston

In 1808, the Buchanan brothers decided to sell the mill, which was brought by J Finlay & co LTD. this business adapted the mill, making extensions in the process. By now, Deanston was a thriving community, which had its original currency, which the local families could use in the shops, which were provided by the mill.

In its heyday, around one thousand people worked in the mill. Many of them living in the village or the surrounding village of Doune. In 1913, Deanston was one of the first villages to be supplied with gaslighting. This was nearly fifty years before the rest of the area that surrounded it.

Unfortunately, due to the decline of the cotton industry, the mill was closed in the middle of the 1960s, leaving the building isolated on and off for approximately 30 years. The company named Burns Stewart, soon brought the building in 1990, to use for their company as whisky manufactures. They would produce Deanston Single Malt Whisky on-site and still do today.

Deanston Distillery

There are several discrepancies in this story. Upon researching the event, we could find no other information that indicated the death of Helen MacDougal or any event that took place in the small village of Deanston. However, the dates of this event fit perfectly into the timeline.

Other stories of Helen MacDougal's whereabouts, takes her all over the United Kingdom to Australia, but there's no other information to back up these claims.

What happened to Margaret Laird?

We know least of what happened to Margaret Laird, who was the wife of William Hare. It is even unknown exactly what date she was released from prison. However, it seems like she did not want to stick around in Edinburgh to wait for the release of her husband.

On the 19th of January 1829, Margaret Laird was seen crossing the North Bridge, holding her baby in her arms. Again, she was recognised and it is claimed that the local mobs began to throw mud bombs and snowballs at her, regardless that she was carrying a small child in her arms. The police stepped in and rescued the now single mother and took her to the watchhouse on Libberton's Wynd.

After a few days of hiding undercover, she made her way to Glasgow, where she was hoping to find a seat on a ship to return her to Ulster in Ireland. However, while in Glasgow, she was seen again and an angry mob crowded around her. Margaret Laird was taken by the local policemen to Carlton watch house in Glasgow for safekeeping. By the 12th of February, she had been taken to Greenock, where she was placed on a ferry that transported her to Belfast. There is no sign of her after this.

What happened to Dr Knox?

Dr Robert Knox chose to keep silent about his dealings with Burke and Hare. He was not questioned during Burke and MacDougal's trial; however, this does not mean he got away with it.

The locals began to riot outside his home and screamed that he should be executed.

His windows were smashed in and his house was vandalised. He continued to employ Edinburgh body-snatchers while lecturing on anatomy. After the Anatomy Act was passed in 1832, his popularity among students decreased. His applications for formal positions in the Edinburgh Medical School were rejected and he began to get pushed out of the school by the other professors.

Eventually, Knox moved to London after the death of his wife. He left his remaining children in the care of his nephew but when he was in London, he was refused to be employed by the local schools. He finally found work at the Cancer Hospital in London Robert Knox began to write some more books and he continued to do this until he passed away in December 1862, at his home at 9 Lambe Terrance in Hackney. He was 71 years old.

Other Books

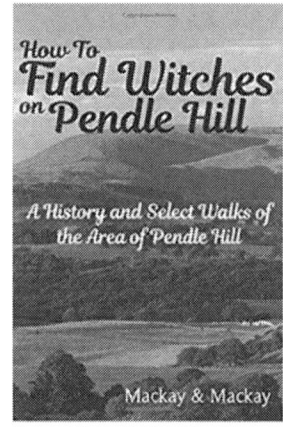

Printed in Great Britain
by Amazon

30414953R00090